PERSPECTIVES

If anyone is puzzled by the subtitle of this book "Intergenerational Missiology," he/she should be informed that "it is a study of inter-generational missions" with the focus on Christological-discipleship, biblical leadership, Kingdom partnerships, respect and loving tender relationship.

In this book, the author skillfully integrated the theoretical frameworks of "Diaspora Missiology" (Joy Tira/Enoch Wan), "Relational Missiology" (Enoch Wan) and "Polycentric Missiology" (Allen Yeh).

This book is regarded as a seminal work within the Lausanne Movement and readers can easily be informed, instructed, and inspired by its rich content and case studies for practical ministries: in bridging the gaps between generations, serving the aging population, and engaging in meaningful Kingdom services in the 21st century context.

Enoch Wan, PhD
Director of PhD|EdD|DIS Programs
Research Professor of Intercultural Studies

Sadiri Joy Tira has offered here an invaluable contribution to the study of intergenerational missiology. His uniqueness includes not only focusing on younger generations, but also older generations who are often the most marginalized and forgotten. He has drawn together an all-star team to expertly weave together biblical theology, personal anecdotes, and the realities of modern global culture. This book is a needed resource in any library!

Allen Yeh, D.Phil
Dean and VP for Academic Affairs
International Theological Seminary/
Learning Synthesis Manager
Lausanne's Generation Conversation

"Missiology is the mother of theology", wrote 19th century theologian Martin Kähler, giving birth to context-specific understandings of God. A context can be geographic or demographic and all followers of Jesus are theologians in our contexts. We are all the result of numerous spiritual mothers and fathers and we are parents to many children growing in the faith. This volume highlights the critical importance of intergenerational relationships for the healthy development of World Christianity. The authors teach us that it requires authenticity, integrity, intentionality, mutual respect, and, above all, biblical fidelity in all that we think, do, and are in Christ. Discipleship is not just taught, it is caught—and this book is essential reading for anyone seeking to be positive influence on the next generation of Jesus' followers in their context for God's glory everywhere.

Jay Mātenga, D.I.S.
Executive Director
WEA Mission Commission

A robust and significant resource for those engaged in missions across the whole life span, *From Womb to Tomb* is the complete package! Edited by someone who has lived his whole life ministering to God's people across ethnic and cultural backgrounds, Dr. Joy Tira has selected contributors (ranging from authors who are famous scholars as well as children!) and carefully curated the topics of this book to reflect the ethos and passion for the fulfillment of the Missio *Dei*.

Nativity A. Petallar, DTh in
Christian Education and Practical Ministry
Associate Dean for PhD Studies
Asia-Pacific Nazarene Theological Seminary

Reading this book *From Womb to Tomb: Intergenerational Missiology in the 21st Century* will help our generation to prevent Judges 2:10 to happen in our time. It is a timely book to read and study for us to understand the Gen Zs, and the Alphas who are shaky in their faith department. This book will remind us of the Nonagenarians, the Babyboomers, the Gen Xs and Ys and their legacies: they are valuable to God who promised of blessings to all generations!

Damples Dulcero-Baclagon, MA
Managing Editor
Asian Missions Advance

Joy Tira is a fascinating man, truly a one of a kind: a brilliant and inquisitive mind, a strong body (prior to his stroke), a determined spirit (even stronger since the stroke), a delightful sense of humor, and a big heart for God, his family, the church and the world!

We are not supposed to have favorites among family members or colleagues on a team. However, I must say that in my years as the Chairman for the Lausanne Movement, Joy Tira was my favorite among the gifted community of Lausanne *Global Catalysts*. He was both – a global thinker and an energetic and productive catalyst. Full of energy, ideas, mischief, and joy!

From Womb to Tomb is another gift from this friend to all who know him, and from all who have joined him in producing it. The contributors he has gathered have given eloquent and instructive expression to the ideas that were forming in Joy's life. For those who know Joy Tira, they will realize this book was not written in a hurry. It is the product of a lifetime of study and reflections and faithfulness in each chapter of his life, and to each generation in his own family. His love for his wife, his pride in his children, his delight in his grandchildren, and his advocacy for older people with whom he and Joy now live, is truly inspiring and instructive.

This book is integral to the vision of the Lausanne Movement: "The Whole Church taking the Whole Gospel to the Whole World."

Douglas Birdsall, PhD
Honorary Chairman
The Lausanne Movement

FROM WOMB TO TOMB

Generational Missiology in the 21st Century and Beyond

Sadiri Joy Tira, Editor

FROM WOMB TO TOMB
Generational Missiology in the 21st Century and Beyond

Copyright © Sadiri Joy Tira, 2024

All rights reserved. No part of this publication may be reproduced, stored in a retrieval system, or transmitted in any form or by any means, electronic, mechanical, photocopying, recording, or otherwise, without written permission of the author and publisher.

This document was originally produced from the Lausanne Generations Conversation [*June/2023*] and is published here with permission. To learn more about the Lausanne Movement, visit WWW.LAUSANNE.ORG and to receive a free Lausanne Global Analysis bimonthly publication, subscribe online at HTTPS://LAUSANNE.ORG/LGA.

Cover design by Henrick Vasquez and Nikita Sushma

Compilation by Damples and Gerry Baclagon

Proofread by
Jade Munsie, Rachel De Lazzer, Marie Osborne, and Mark Hedinger

Published by Sadiri Joy Tira, Edmonton, Canada

ISBN:
    Paperback 978-1-77354-585-1
    ebook 978-1-77354-586-8

Publication assistance and digital printing in Canada by

PageMaster
PUBLISHING
PageMaster.ca

Dedication

*To the Manding-Tira tribe,
Dimangondayao Family,
and Manuel Family*

***"Lord, throughout the generations
you have been our home!"
(Psalm 90:1)***

ACKNOWLEDGEMENTS:

SINCERE AND DEEP GRATITUDE TO:

- Contributing Writers from the oldest to youngest
- Book Endorsers
- Editorial Team and Graphic Designers
- Proof Readers
- Prayer Supporters
- The Publishers

"Your labour in the Lord is not in vain" (I Corinthians 15:58)

Gratis et Amore

Sadiri Joy B. Tira
Editor
May 10, 2024

Contents

Foreword 1
Preface 3
Introduction 6

I. Biblical Contextual Intergenerational Missions 9
Psalmists on Generational Mission 10
Biblical Foundations: Life and Leadership of Moses, Joshua and Caleb 21
An Intergenerational Partnership; the Story of Ruth and Naomi 39
Intergenerational Mission in the New Testament: Examples of Life-on-Life Modeling by Jesus and Paul 47

II. Sociological, Anthropological, Theological, And Missiological Aspects of Intergenerational Mission 65
Engaging the Next Generation in God's Global Mission 66
Bridging the Gap: Embracing Intergenerational Leadership in Christian Ministry 78

III. Case Studies 91
Out of the Mouths of Babes: God Speaking in the Lives of Children 92
Being a Tsinoy Gen Z: Struggling With Language, Hybridity, And Identity 96
Investing Across Generations: a Personal Reflection 104
He Remains Faithful: Reflections of a Baby Boomer 112
Family Tragedy to Triumph: Pursuit of a Diaspora Eurasian (an Interview With Nonagenarian) 123
The Centenarian: Receiving Their Personal Legacy 129

IV. Pastoral Exhortation 133
Intergenerational Mission: Passing Our Faith Legacy to the Next Generations 134
Do Not Abuse Seniors Nor Exclude Us From the Family Circle 154

Conclusion 159
Afterword 160
List of Contributors 162
Appendix 167

Foreword

Nana Yaw Offei Awuku

Filipino-born global citizen and babyboomer Sadiri Joy Tira will forever be a shining inspiration and witness to the beauty of Christian faith, faithfulness, friendship, and fruitfulness for many generations worldwide. This book is a testament to Joy's life, love, leadership, and legacy, weaving together a unique tapestry of multi-disciplinary perspectives.

Diaspora missiology is a subject that brings joy wherever Joy Tira is mentioned in global mission. In 2017, at a strategic Lausanne Leadership meeting held on the historic campus of Wheaton College, USA, Joy Tira approached me and a few friends, saying in his characteristic cheerful yet challenging tone, "Lausanne must think younger and younger." I immediately understood his emphasis on the importance of younger generations.

This outstanding book by cherished friends, colleagues, scholars, and expert practitioners in diaspora and generational missiology reveals Joy Tira's Great Commission heart for reaching the ends of the earth globally and the end of the age generationally. This unique perspective on Jesus' co-mission to make disciples of all nations (to the ends of the earth) and to the end of the age (all generations) is often missed by many pastors, mission practitioners, professors, and professionals.

Joy Tira, the emeritus cheerleader of diasporan missiology and champion of generations mission, captures God's heartbeat in the title "From Womb to Tomb." This book is a must-read for everyone who cares about God's mission in a strategic, sustainable, and Spirit-inspired way.

As I write this foreword, I hold firm convictions on why this generational imperative of global mission is more urgent today and needs the priority attention of the global church:

- More generations are alive and living together today than ever in history, with seven generations sharing our global community spaces. We urgently need fresh attention to healthy and hopeful generational neighboring.
- Families and faith communities provide the broadest natural environments for multi-generations to co-habitate, and workplaces and schools to build or break communities across generations.
- Our global human community meets as generational neighbors in a shared journey of life transitions, and our inter-generational interaction and peaceful engagements are crucial for a healthy and hopeful community.
- The world population has quadrupled from 2 billion to 8 billion between 1925 and 2023, with more grandparents and grandchildren at home and in the workplace than ever. This generational bulge demands attention.
- A peaceful and progressive global community will be hopeful only if we learn to live, love, lead together across generations, impacting a legacy of blessing from generation to generation. This is an urgent call, a generational commission, and a common global concern.

As Psalm 78:1-7 reminds us, each generation should set its hope anew on God, not forgetting his glorious miracles and obeying his commands. Let us listen attentively, live purposely, and may the fruit of our legacy last to bless many more generations – in true obedience to Christ, by the power of the Holy Spirit, and for the glory of the Father!

Nana Yaw Offei Awuku
Global Director of Generations,
Lausanne Movement
Based in Ghana

Preface

Sadiri Joy Tira

I decided to assemble this volume as a result of the inspiration of a godly man from Ghana, Africa, who subsequently became a friend and co-pilgrim. Together, we embarked on a journey from the City of Man to the City of God. In 2016, I first met Reverend Nana Yaw Offei Awuku at the Lausanne Younger Leaders Forum held in Jakarta. Our brief encounter was followed by a face-to-face meeting in Chicago, and closer interactions in Wittenberg, Germany in 2017, when a select group of 70 global missions leaders met for consultation. I recall walking with him to the Castle Temple, where the great German reformer Martin Luther was laid to rest over 500 years ago. In one of our sessions, I heard him praying for younger leaders who would one day take the baton of leadership.

My spirit was stirred, and I was moved when Nana prayed. I thought that when a preacher preached, he spoke to people. However, when the man of God was praying, he was speaking with God! And no wonder I was deeply moved; it was because he knows God--the Triune God! Soon after these events, he was appointed by the Lausanne Movement as the Global Associate Director for Generations. He leads the younger leaders. His passion for the future of younger leaders is contagious.

The title of this book, *From Womb to Tomb: Generational Missiology in the 21st Century and Beyond*, refers to the human journey from birth to death. The journey begins in the Womb and ends in the Tomb (grave).

WOMB AND TOMB?

The historic Roe V. Wade's abortion case in the USA was decided over 50 years ago. As the consequence of the case, how many children were denied the opportunity to live in a home? How many have not enjoyed riding a bike to school or church, or reading and singing the Christmas story? The womb should be regarded as the most sacred and safest place, not a place of death, while the tomb is the ultimate destiny and the final resting place.

God said to Jeremiah, *"Before I formed you in the womb I knew you, before you were born I set you apart; I appointed you as a prophet to the nations."* (1:5)

Like the Prophet Jeremiah, we are formed in our mother's womb and there, God made us in the secret place; he knew us and wove our whole lives together in the depths of the earth (Psalm 139: 15-16).

I am fascinated by tombs. During my tenure as a pastor in Edmonton, Alberta, Canada, I made a habit of visiting cemeteries during my days off. During late summer and early autumn seasons, I would visit these places to read the grave markers and find out who had died and been buried there. Some were great academics, lawyers, scholars, priests, businessmen, or athletes.

Regardless of their achievements, education, or careers, they had all died and been buried there. The number of graves exceeds that of monuments.

THE BIBLE HAS A LOT TO SAY ABOUT TOMBS (AND GRAVES).

Tombs are places of rest for prophets, warriors, and kings.

Jesus Christ, the King of Kings, was buried in the tomb provided by Joseph of Arimathea. *"Later, Joseph of Arimathea asked Pilate for the body of Jesus.... Taking Jesus' body, [Joseph and Arimathea and Nicodemus] wrapped it, with the spices, in strips of linen. ... At the place where Jesus was crucified, there was a garden, and in the garden a new tomb, in which no one had ever been laid.*" (John 19:38-42) The tomb was a significant place for Jesus.

In 2006, the former chairman of the Lausanne Movement, Reverend Doug Birdsall, and I were in Macau, China. We visited the tomb of Robert Morrison, the first missionary to China. At the burial place, Rev. Birdsall appointed me to be the first Senior Associate/Catalyst of Lausanne for Diasporas. There are other significant tombs I have also visited, including Mother Teresa's in Kolkata, India, and the graves of Billy and Ruth Graham in Charlotte, North Carolina, USA. Every time I visit Manila, the Philippines, I pay my respects at the burial places of my parents. I am assured and hopeful that these tombs and graves will be opened when Jesus comes again.

This new book is regarded as a seminal work within the Lausanne Movement. However, in a report published on January 26, 2011, entitled: "Lausanne Movement Releases Cape Town Commitment," Lindsey Brown, the International Director of the Lausanne Movement, stated "Each generation needs to restate the biblical gospel for its own time. We have sought to bring clarity to the essentials of the Gospel, and to express them in a fresh way in our generation."

The authors of this book are multi-ethnic and multi-national, as well as interdisciplinary scholars and inter-generational men and women. Their common denominator is that they know Jesus and are followers of Him. Their collective goal is to assist in the fulfillment of the Great Commission.

Sadiri Joy Tira
Edmonton, Alberta Canada
May 15, 2024

Introduction

Sadiri Joy Tira

Missiology is simply the academic study of Christian Mission, and the practice of Christian Missions for the building and growth of the Global Church of Jesus Christ (Tira).

What is this "Generational Missiology" ?

Missiologists "they are academic invaders" ! I remembered my professor - Friend, the late Dr Samuel Larsen told me over (a cup of coffee) and other students at Reformed Theological Seminary (RTS) in Jackson, Mississippi. He said: "Missiology is academically bankrupt, all the Missiologists do well is to invade other disciplines to borrow their theories, methodologies, research questions and findings!"

For example:

They don't understand culture so they go to Anthropology; they don't understand society so they go to Sociology; they do not have a World Map -that belongs to Geography; they don't understand human behavior so they ask the Psychologist; they don't know how to properly count numbers, that belongs to math/statistics; they don't know how to look for money, they ask for help from business people and economists; they don't know how to interpret the Bible that belongs to Biblical Hermeneutics; they don't know God that belongs to Theology!

All they have are: the great commandment and commission of their Master, Jesus Christ!

I thought that was funny but true. Missiologists are great interdisciplinary students.

This book, From *Womb to Tomb: Generational Missiology in the 21st Century and Beyond* is the product by multidisciplinary scholars and practitioners of Mission.

There are four main parts

1. Biblical and Contextual Theology: the book of Psalms is rich in generational expression, the life of Moses, Joshua, Caleb are examples of Inter-Generational leadership; Ruth and Naomi must be understood in our 21st century Context as the model of Biblical partnership and gender friendship of diaspora women, while the model of Jesus and Paul are unchanging. It is relevant to all generations globally.
2. Sociological and Anthropological and Missiological - this chapter includes portraits of the new global missions landscape. The authors focused on the Global Youth Culture and their potential as "mission force Kingdom builders." However, it is vital to understand their cultural struggles and needs and behaviors for effective missions work.
3. Several Case Studies are included for the readers to (hear or read). True to life inter-generational journey from Gen A, Gen Z, Millennials, Boomers and Nona-Genarian Diaspora, Asian and North American hybrids and child of second generation immigrant.
4. Lastly, The Pastoral Exhortations are included for Jesus' parishioners; His parish is Global and trans-generational!

Generational Missiology is a study of Inter-generational missions. Its tenets are Christological-discipleship, biblical leadership, kingdom partnerships, respect and loving tender relationship!

To be noted in this volume are the work of evangelical missiologists and strategists: Polycentric missiology (Yeh) and Diaspora Missiology (Tira/Wan) and Relational Missiology (Wan) when cross pollinated will produce effective Generational Missiology. This Generational Missiology is inter-generational, global intercultural, diasporic and hybrid, cross pollinated driven by Digital Technology (Tira. 2024).

REFERENCES:

Handley, Joseph. *PolyCentric Mission Leadership*. Regnum, 2022.

Pantoja, Tira & Wan. *Scattered: The Filipino Global Presence*. Life Change, 2004.

Tira & Uytanlet. *A Hybrid World: Diaspora Hybridity and Missio Dei*. WCP: 2020.

Tira & Wan. *Missions in Action in the 21st Century*. Filipino International Network & Institute of Diaspora Studies/ Western Seminary, 2008.

Tira & Wan. *Missions in Practice in the 21st Century*. William Carey International University Press, 2010.

Tira & Yamamori. *SCATTERED and GATHERED: A Global Compendium of Diaspora Missiology*, Langham 2020.

Yeh, Allen. *PolyCentric Missiology. 21st Century Mission From Everyone to Everywhere*, IVF Press. 2016.

I.
Biblical Contextual Intergenerational Missions

Psalmists on Generational Mission

Joseph Shao

Psalm 61:6 is a powerful verse that reads, "Increase the days of the king's life, his years for many generations." While this verse may seem focused on the longevity of David's reign as a king, it holds a deeper meaning that resonates with the concept of generational mission. What is the purpose of asking God for long life? The phrase "many generations" (*dor wador*) literally means "generations to generations." It implies a continuity that extends beyond an individual's lifetime, suggesting a legacy that not only spans from womb (birth) to tomb (death), but also the wombs to tombs of many generations after David. In this discourse, we delve into the implications of this biblical truth on the generational mission of individuals, families, and communities. We will also present the important truths of Psalms 71, 78, 90 and 145, as the psalmists pray and retell their faith journey to the younger generations.

In the context of faith and spirituality, we will explore the importance of the intentional transferring of faith to many generations. The idea of generational mission in the 21st century and beyond encompasses the responsibility and privilege of passing down faith, values, and spiritual principles from one generation to the next. A biblical worldview sees life with a clear meaning and purpose.

UNDERSTANDING GENERATIONAL MISSION

1. ROOTED IN FAITH

The journey from womb to tomb signifies the entirety of human life. To embark on a generational mission means laying a foundation of faith that starts early in life and continues until the end. Faith becomes the guiding force that shapes perspectives, decisions, and actions across multiple generations. Our Almighty God is not only the God of Abraham, Isaac, and Jacob, he is also the God of David and those descendants after him!

The journey begins in the womb where life is conceived and formed. The purpose of one's life takes root. Psalm 139 beautifully captures the intricacies of this divine craftsmanship, emphasizing God's intimate involvement in shaping each person. David in Psalm 139 expresses his faith beginning from his mother's womb. God's personal initiative in caring for a person starts in the womb (see Job 10:11; Ps. 119:73). As David articulates his experience with the omniscience of God (Ps. 139:1-6) and omnipresence of God (Ps. 139:7-12), he expresses that God had a purpose in creating him even as he was in his mother's womb (Ps. 139:13). The idea of creation points to an acknowledgement of God's omnipresent, and also to the concept that the existence of man belongs to God and not to himself. Even as an embryo, his spiritual and physical being are fearfully and wonderfully made. David states how as an unborn with his frame "made in a secret place" and his "unformed body," the Lord had written them in his book (Ps. 139:14-16). It denotes that all his days are mapped out in advance. Every detail of his life points to God's presence and omnificent care. From pre-natal fashioning by God, he goes to the tomb with God's planning even at his embryonic stages in his mother's womb. God has a distinct blueprint and clear purpose for him. This thoughtful idea is very similar to Jeremiah, as he expresses his call to ministry. The Lord shaped him in his mother's womb and set him apart with a clear mission (Jer. 1:5). The divine plan for Jeremiah to be a prophet for the nations starts at his fetal development. Understanding one's purpose and calling from an early stage sets the trajectory for a life dedicated to fulfilling a generational mission.

2. OBEDIENCE AND LONG LIFE

The petition of David to prolong his life should be traced back to the teaching of Moses in his addresses to the new generation after their sojourn in the wilderness. In Moses' first address, acknowledging God's deliverance (Deut. 1:1-4:43), he appeals to the new generation to obey God's command wholeheartedly (Deut. 4:1-2, 5). Moses focuses on who God is and what he has done as the motivation for their obedience. As long as they live, they need to revere God and to teach the next generation (Deut. 4:9-10). Remember, this is a new generation after the 40 years of sojourn in *Kadesh Barnea* wilderness. Repeatedly Moses reminds them,

> *"Keep his decrees and commands, which I am giving you today, so that it may go well with you and your children after you and that you may live long in the land the LORD your God gives you for all time"* (Deut. 4:40, Italics mine).

Obedience to God in keeping his teaching prompts the blessings of wellness and long life for the present generation and for those descendants after them. Hence, long life in the land and the covenantal blessings for the younger generations are directly related to the transmission of faith.

In the second address of Moses (Deut. 4:44-28:68), he likewise stresses the blessing of long life as a motivation for obedience with their response to God's teaching. Faithfulness would bring life, well-being, as well as the prolonging of life (Deut. 5:33). It is for the parents, as well as generations after them. He continues to instruct them,

"These are the commands, decrees and laws the LORD your God directed me to teach you to observe in the land that you are crossing the Jordan to possess, so that you, your children and their children after them may fear the LORD your God as long as you live by keeping all his decrees and commands that I give you, and so that you may enjoy long life. Hear, Israel, and be careful to obey so that it may go well with you and that you may increase greatly in a land flowing with milk and honey, just as the LORD, the God of your ancestors, promised you" (Deut. 6:1-3).

God's teaching is directed to both the parents, as well as the generations after them. The Law (Torah) of Moses, consisting of "commands, decrees and laws," is the teaching of the Lord for his people. The entire community is responsible to let their lives be shaped by the Torah.[1] Here again in Deuteronomy 6:2, the potential that the "days may be long," is directly related to their response to God's teaching. The promise of patriarchal blessings is fulfilled as they walk with the Lord (Deut. 6:3). The idea of the ability to live long entails living under God's care and guidance.

The heart of Israel's confession in Deuteronomy 6:4-9 is that the Lord alone is the God of Israel. Israel must worship Him alone. Secondly, Israel itself is a unity. The people's oneness includes those whom Moses addresses and those generations that come after him. Parents should diligently teach their offspring and continually talk about God's will. On the other hand, the younger generations need to identify with their ancestors and participate in the memory and in faith of God's deliverance in history.[2] Thirdly, the people must love the Lord with all their heart, their soul, and their strength. Since

---

1 John Goldingay, *Old Testament Theology. Vol 2: Israel Faith* (Downers Grove: IVP Academic, 2006), 189.

2 Every New Year's Eve, our extended family would gather. My dad, Rev. Wesley K. Shao, being the eldest of the Shao clan in Manila, Philippines, would always remind us about our family's spiritual history. Two women missionaries went to TongAn, Fujian, China and led my grandfather to Christ. Since then, the Shao clan continues to follow the Lord.

obedience to the Lord is the foundation of every family's happiness, the commandments of Moses need to be engraved in the hearts of the present generation and carefully taught and passed on to future generations by grandparents and parents (Deut. 6:20-25; 11:19).

The last act of Moses before his death, with Joshua besides him, was Moses again encouraging the people of God,

> *"Take to heart all the words by which I am warning you today, that you may command them to your children, that they may be careful to do all the words of this law. For it is no empty word for you, but your very life, and by this word you shall live long in the land that you are going over the Jordan to possess"* (Deut. 32:46-47; Italics mine).

Take note that "the words of this law (Torah)" is the same as "all the words" of Moses. Long life is a blessing, more so with a responsibility for transmitting faith to the younger generations.

The addresses of Moses and his last act is for the next generation to live a long life and have meaningful communication with the younger generation to obey the Lord. Thus, long life has a generational mission!

3. EXPERIENCING GOD AND THE ROLE OF PARENTS

Parents play a pivotal role in transferring faith to the next generations. They serve as the primary influences and educators to their children, creating an environment where faith is not just taught but lived. Modeling a life of faith involves intentional actions, consistent values, and an atmosphere of love and grace. This is exactly the life David lived before God as can be seen in Psalm 61.

David, in his cry for desperation, implores God to listen to his prayer. He requests God to lead him to the rock that is higher than him (Ps. 61:2). The rock is a metaphor for protection, security, and refuge (see Ps. 27:5). Since David has experienced him as a refuge,

God is his strong and reliable tower of a fortress (Ps. 61:3). He longs to dwell in God's tent forever, to find protective care under his wings (Ps. 61:4). Mentioning of rock, refuge, tower, and tents all points to his reliance on God. Amidst life's trials and tribulations, David finds solace in the shelter of God's presence. Only God can be a refuge for him from the storms of life. David shares his own experiences of seeking God's protection. David invites future generations to find their strength and security in God alone. The prayer offers a timeless message of hope and assurance to those who will come after him.

As a part of the people of God, David would have learned many spiritual lessons as a son of Jesse. Outwardly, it may seem that David in his early years, as the youngest son of Jesse, was hardly accepted by his own family members. Even as Samuel came to the family with the purpose to anoint a king-designate, he was not initially asked to be present at the anointing (1 Sam. 16:11-12). As a young unknown warrior, he drew his faith from what he learned in the family as well as his experience as a shepherd (1 Sam. 17:32-37). His faith in God motivated him to share his faith in the book of Psalms. David's faith can be seen in many of the psalms that he had written. It can be seen too from other psalms that were dedicated to him. David also passed on his spiritual legacy to Solomon, and his descendants through the Davidic covenant (2 Sam.7). David's desire to serve and please God and his complete dependence on God were an example of faith, and he became a model for Judah's future kings.

David's example of loving God is a great teaching for the generational mission. We need to pass on our faith to the next generation through our daily example and teaching. Before his death, David gave Solomon a direct verbal teaching to follow the Lord,

"..you may prosper in all you do and wherever you go, and the Lord may keep his promises to me: 'If your descendants watch how they live, and if they walk faithfully before me with all their heart and soul, you will never fail to have a man on the throne of Israel'" (1 Kgs. 2:3-4).

David's heart was to "obey the Lord his God with sincerity" (1 Kgs. 15:3), which was the standard for the king of Judah to serve the Lord. In 1 Chronicles 28, David gives instructions to the leaders of the tribes of Israel to build the temple. But most importantly, he commands his son Solomon to follow and serve God wholeheartedly (1 Chron. 28:9-10). Solomon would not carry out this building task alone, for God himself would "search" (darash) Solomon's heart. As a result, Solomon sought God. David encouraged his son to take positive action. David had a close relationship with God and taught his son Solomon to serve God wholeheartedly. He was a good example for generational mission. We need to keep reminding the younger generation to love the Lord!

IMPLEMENTING GENERATIONAL MISSION

In the tapestry of human existence, the transmission of faith from one generation to another generation stands as a sacred thread, weaving through time, connecting the past, present and future. This enduring act of passing down beliefs, values, and spiritual wisdom is paramount in the journey of humanity. In the Psalms, specifically Psalms 71, 78, 90, and 145, we find profound insights into the significance and methodology of transmitting faith to successive generations.

1. A PRAYER FOR ENDURING FAITH (PSALM 71)

Psalm 71 emerges as a heartfelt prayer for God's protection and deliverance in the face of adversity. The psalmist declares, "Even when I am old and gray, do not forsake me, my God, till I declare your power to the next generation, your mighty acts to all who are to come" (Ps. 71:17). Here, we witness a profound commitment to transmitting faith to future generations, even in the twilight years of life.

In transmitting faith through Psalm 71, the psalmist embodies a spirit of perseverance and trust in God's faithfulness. By entrusting their spiritual legacy to the next generation, the psalmist demonstrates a profound understanding of the interconnectedness of past, present, and future. Through the act of declaring God's mighty acts, the psalmist invites future generations to embrace their role as stewards of faith, carrying forward the torch of spiritual wisdom for generations to come.

2. THE POWER OF RETELLING IN PASSING ON FAITH (PSALM 78)

Psalm 78 is a powerful testament to the role of storytelling in the transmission of faith. The psalmist exhorts the listeners to "tell the next generation the praiseworthy deeds of the LORD, his power, and the wonders he has done" (Ps. 78:4). It is also the duty of the next generation to teach "the children yet to be born, and they in turn would tell their children" (Ps. 78:6). The purpose of retelling is for generations after generations to "put their trust in God" (Ps. 78:7). The recounting of God's faithfulness throughout history serves not only to preserve the collective memory of his actions but also to inspire future generations to have faith. Each generation must pass on its sacred traditions to the next in accordance with the will of God and avoid the mistakes of the past generation.

Focusing on Ephraim (the tribe of Joseph) with their special status and prominence (Ps. 78:9), the psalmist retells the redemptive actions of God (Ps 78:12-16; 40-55).[3] Sad to say, they did not keep God's covenant. They did not remain faithful to God. Instead, they rebelled against God in the wilderness (Ps. 78:17-20), and in the land (Ps. 78:56-58). Eventually the Lord chose the tribe of Judah as the leader (Ps. 78:65-72). The psalmist reiterates God's graciousness, but each act resulted in specific instances of Israel's failure, and these instances were undeserved. It would have been different if God's

---

[3] The date of Psalm 78 cannot be pinpointed, but it is certainly possible for this psalm to be used and reused in the community, reminding them to retell the historical story to each generation. See Nancy L. deClassse-Watford, Rolf A. Jacobson, and Beth LaNeel Tanner, *The Book of Psalms*. NICOT (Grand Rapids: Eerdmans, 2014), 621.

people not only trusted in God's deeds and teachings, but also taught the next generation.

Through storytelling, faith ceases to be abstract doctrine and becomes a living narrative—a tapestry of divine intervention, human frailty, and redemption. The psalmist underscores the importance of engaging the senses, employing vivid imagery and metaphor to captivate the imagination of the listeners. From the time of the Israelite exodus, to their experience of God's parting of the Red Sea under Moses' leadership, to the election of David as the shepherd of his people, each story serves as a beacon of hope, illuminating the path of faith for generations to come.

3. THE ETERNAL NATURE OF GOD'S FAITHFULNESS (PSALM 90)

The grand prayer of Moses in Psalm 90 is a great illustration of how a parent can pray to God on behalf of their children. Moses reflects on the eternal nature of God and the transient nature of humanity. Moses affirms that the Lord is their dwelling place from "generations to generations" (*dor wador*; Ps. 90:1). This acknowledgment of God's perpetual presence underscores the foundational truth that faith is not confined to a single era but endures across time.

In his prayer of supplication, Moses petitions God to bestow the continuity of his steadfast love. It is for *"all our days," "many days"* and *"many years"* (Ps. 90:14-17). He asks for the work of God to be manifest, and his splendor to be revealed to the future generations (Ps. 90:16). It is a great prayer requesting God to show his inconceivable glory and eternal beauty to generations who may not have experienced his greatness during the wilderness.

In transmitting faith, the recognition of God's eternal and glorious nature becomes a cornerstone. Just as God has been faithful to past generations, so too can future generations find solace and strength in his unwavering love and constancy. We are tasked with imparting this timeless truth to those who come after us, instilling in them a sense of God's unchanging character.

4. THE GENERATIONAL PRAISE OF GOD'S GREATNESS (PSALM 145)

Psalm 145 is a resounding hymn of praise, celebrating the greatness and goodness of God in universal care. The psalmist declares, "One generation commends your works to another, they tell of your mighty acts" (Ps. 145:4). This psalm is an acrostic psalm praising the greatness and glory of the Lord. The using of the 22 letters of the Hebrew alphabet extolling God's awesome works expresses a thorough praise of God.

The psalmist explores God's greatness as infinite and awe-inspiring. Each generation has certain memories, stories, and values that they want to pass on to the next generation, and more importantly, share those experiences with their children and grandchildren. It cannot be assumed that children and grandchildren will automatically continue the faith of their grandparents and parents in the Lord. The transmittal of faith must be continuously renewed with each generation. Every generation must be reminded who God is and what he has done for humanity. Here, we encounter the cyclical nature of faith transmission—a continuous flow of adoration and testimony passed from one generation to the next.

Central to the psalmist's exaltation is the recognition of God's multifaceted nature. His sovereignty, compassion, and faithfulness endure throughout all generations. In transmitting faith, we are called not only to recount God's acts of worship, prayer, and service, but to also cultivate a legacy of praise, inviting future generations to join in the chorus of adoration and thanksgiving.

THE IMPERATIVE OF INTERGENERATIONAL FAITH TRANSMISSION

In the synthesis of what psalmists teach us, we find a compelling imperative for intergenerational faith transmission. As stewards of faith, we are entrusted with the sacred task of nurturing the spiritual growth of those who follow in our footsteps. This responsibility transcends mere instruction; it requires authentic engagement, vulnerability, and relational investment.

At its core, transmitting faith is an act of love—a testament to our desire to see future generations flourish in their relationship with God. It demands humility, recognizing that we are but custodians of a faith that spans the ages. It requires intentionality, creating spaces for dialogue, mentorship, and shared experience. And it necessitates perseverance, knowing that the seeds we sow today will bear fruit in the generations to come.

In conclusion, these teachings in psalms offer profound insights into the sacred journey of transmitting faith to future generations. From seeking refuge in God's shelter (Ps. 61) to a prayer of enduring faith (Ps 71), from the power of remembering and retelling to the generational praise of his greatness (Ps. 78), to embracing the eternal nature of God's faithfulness (Ps. 90), and to the inter-generational praise of God's greatness (Ps. 145), these psalms invite us to participate in a timeless narrative of faith and redemption. As we heed the call to pass down the torch of faith, may we do so with grace, humility, and unwavering hope, trusting in the promise that God's faithfulness endures to all generations.

Biblical Foundations: Life and Leadership of Moses, Joshua and Caleb

Joy V. Recla

In this paper, we are going to look at three biblical figures Moses, Joshua and Caleb, to explore their formation towards becoming great leaders. In the Old Testament, our primary source of exploration, we will find a glimpse of their family background, significant people around them, their experiences and exploits that helped shaped each of them to become the influential leader that they came to be.

MOSES

THE BEGINNINGS

It was under these harsh conditions in a foreign land that Moses was born to slave parents. Instead of delight in having given birth to a newborn baby boy, his mother and father would have been mortified at the thought that this baby will be murdered, if discovered.

This information on the early life of Moses comes primarily from the first half of the Book of Exodus. In chapter 1, we learn that the Israelites who had immigrated to Egypt because of a famine had become fruitful and numerous. And because of that, they had become a threat to the Pharaoh, the ruler of Egypt at that time who consequentially enslaved them and ordered the killing of their baby boys, two years old and under. We find that Moses' mother was ingenious in thinking of a way to save her baby. She put him in a basket and floated him on the Nile River. Whether it was fortuitous or by timed strategy, just when the daughter of Pharaoh was bathing in the Nile, the baby in the basket floated by. She must have recognized this baby as a Hebrew child who was among those who Pharaoh, her father, ordered to be killed. Yet, she showed favor on the child and his family, and did not turn over the baby to be killed; instead, she took him under her care and protection.

It was also perfectly timed that Moses' sister was in the vicinity when the princess looked for someone to take care of the baby and nurse him on her behalf. In the end, Moses' own mother got to care and nurture her own son. Moses' life was not only spared, but he received the provisions of the palace until he was a grown man. More so, he was nourished in his own household, and taught the values and beliefs of his own family. Surely, we can attribute this to the providential guidance and orchestration of God in Moses' life. So, at an early phase of his life, Moses already had two sets of adults to care for him, and two sets of cultural values to shape him.

GROWING UP YEARS AND RELIGIOUS FORMATION

We do not know much about Moses' growing up years. But we know that as a young child, he was raised in his own home by his own parents. Surely, his parents taught him their values and beliefs, and passed on to him their faith in Yahweh, the God of Israel. We can assume that his faith in Yahweh, his religious convictions and spiritual values were shaped in his own home under the guidance and influence of his own parents.

On the other hand, we also know that Moses also belonged to an Egyptian household. This Egyptian household did not only consist of his mother and her servants, but also of other members of the royal household. "Evidence seems to show that most families were multi-generational, and the household consisted of parents and children along with grandparents, and often aunts. Sometimes it's confusing for modern scholars to figure out the exact relationships in ancient Egyptian families because terms for family members from different generations were not distinguished."[4]

From what we know about ancient Egypt, children were considered important, and so were cared for and taught well. Good mothers took good care of their children.[5] They also had values that differentiated good from bad. Then, there were other members of that household who were part of the family, and then there were also slaves. All these individuals must have had a share of time and opportunity to influence Moses.[6]

And since Moses grew up within a royal household, it could be assumed that he received the best care and tutelage not only from his adoptive mother but also from the tutors in the palace.

BECOMING A GREAT LEADER

Early Crisis: Next thing we know, he was already an adult engaging with the Egyptian slave masters who were oppressing his people. In this first incident that the biblical narrator narrates about Moses' adult life, we are made aware that Moses identified with the Israelites as "his people," and that he was passionate and cared about their plight. "He looked upon the burdens and saw an Egyptian beating

---

[4] Lisa K. Sabbahy, *Daily Life of Women in Ancient Egypt*. The Greenwood Press: Santa Barbara, California (2022), pp. 1-2
[5] Sabbahy, *Daily Life of Women*, p. 14
[6] Ibid.

a Hebrew, one of his people." (Exod. 2:11) Moved by the suffering of his people and the injustice that they were enduring, he took matters into his own hands and struck down the Egyptian. At the same time that he was fighting against injustice, he also was aware that killing the Egyptian was wrong. This is evidence by the fact that he hid the Egyptian in the sand to cover up for what he had done wrong. We see a clash in his identity and values. He was an Israelite, yet raised as the Egyptian princess' son. He saw the oppression of his people and took action, yet he also knew that the action he took was wrong.

YEARS OF HIBERNATION

Realizing his wrong doing, and being most likely confused about whom he should turn to, he escaped to the wilderness where he would end up spending 40 years of his life. While nothing notable happened to him there in terms of fighting against the injustice suffered by his people, these forty years would end being his years of preparation for the great mission that God was to call him to, that of liberating his people from slavery and oppression.

It was during this time that he met his wife, Zipporah (Exod. 3:1), and became integrated with a Midianite household. His father-in-law, Jethro, must have also influenced him a lot in terms of leading and caring for his family and also in the principles of religious leadership. Jethro was a priest of Midian (Exod. 18:1), who had established himself and his family in Midian, an area stretching along the eastern edge of the Gulf of Aqaba in northwestern Arabia. We know that Jethro taught him one of the best principles of leadership and management that Moses applied when he was already leading a large community of Israelites through the wilderness enroute to the Promise Land. After the Israelites' exodus from Egypt, while they were encamped at Sinai, Jethro visited Moses and saw the daunting responsibilities he had, he commented to Moses that what he was doing for the people is not good. "What is this you are doing for the people? Why do you alone sit as judge, while all these people stand around you from morning till evening?" (Exod. 18:14)

Jethro then counsels Moses with a great counsel that even all leaders should know. Moses needs to identify his priorities and learn to delegate. He told Moses that his responsibility is to meet with God and bring the people's disputes to God. His task was to take God's instructions and teach the people how to live and behave. But Moses should not be the one to sit and judge over every dispute the people had with each other. Instead, he should select capable, trustworthy men who fear God and appoint them over groups of Israelites, to serve as judges. They should be the one who would judge simple cases. Only the more difficult cases should be elevated to Moses. This would help Moses to not be overwhelmed with an onslaught of cases to settle, and thus would be able to focus on his most important task of leading the nation to the Promise Land. So, we see Moses receiving very important guidance and counsel from another "parent-figure" who was not from among his own household or people. This time, it is from a Midianite; also descendants of Abraham, but not Hebrews (Gen. 25: 1-4).

RESPONDING TO GOD'S CALL

It was also in the wilderness that Moses received his call from God for the great task of leading the Israelites out of Egypt. In the mundanity of his regular day just tending over the flock, something spectacular happened when Moses encountered God in a burning bush. In this encounter, he learned at least two things about God: 1) that God was also concerned about the plight of his people, and 2) that this God who was concerned about his people was a holy God. What are the implications of these two realizations? Firstly, the people he considered "his people" were ultimately God's people (Exodus 3:10, "my people"). And since they were God's people, He had heard their cry and had the intention to liberate them from their suffering and oppression. This agenda would be something that Moses could relate with. Secondly, the fact that God is holy meant that there was no impurity, deceit or malice in God. It meant that He could be trusted. Yet, Moses hesitated. He saw three problems: 1) he did not know how he would introduce God to his people; 2) he was ill-equipped for the task; 3) Pharaoh was a powerful foe to come against. All these obstacles were dealt with. God gave Moses His name and identity. Moses was given powerful signs and a strategy to handle the task. And though Pharaoh was powerful, he was no match to the unformidable power of God.

ACCEPTING THE CHALLENGE

Eventually, Moses was persuaded to accept the challenging task God has called him to. It was not easy and there were a lot of obstacles to overcome on the way to accomplishing the mission given him, both internally in his own household, and externally, among the people and with Pharaoh. Eventually, he was able to successfully lead the Israelites out of Egypt. Though he was not able to successfully bring them into the Promise land, it was his assistant Joshua, primarily trained by him, who completed the task that he started.

PASSING ON THE FAITH

It must have been the failure of the first generation to enter the Promise Land, as well as his own exclusion from entering it, that led Moses to emphasize in his last sermons to the Israelites the importance of faith and of parents passing down their faith to their children.

Deuteronomy 4:8-9

And what great nation is there, that has statutes and rules so righteous as all this law that I set before you today? Only take care, and keep your soul diligently, lest you forget the things that your eyes have seen, and lest they depart from your heart all the days of your life. Make them known to your children and your children's children.

Deuteronomy 6:7

You shall teach them [God's words] diligently to your children, and shall talk of them when you sit in your house, and when you walk by the way, and when you lie down, and when you rise.

Deuteronomy 6:20-25

When your son asks you in time to come, 'What is the meaning of the testimonies and the statutes and the rules that the LORD our God has commanded you?' then you shall say to your son, 'We were Pharaoh's slaves in Egypt. And the LORD brought us out of Egypt with a mighty hand. And the LORD showed signs and wonders, great and grievous, against Egypt and against Pharaoh and all his household, before our eyes. And he brought us out from there, that he might bring us in and give us the land that he swore to give to our fathers. And the LORD commanded us to do all these statutes, to fear the LORD our God, for our good always, that he might preserve us alive, as we are this day. And it will be righteousness for us, if we are careful to do all this commandment before the LORD our God, as he has commanded us.'

Deuteronomy 11:19

You shall teach them [God's words] to your children, talking of them when you are sitting in your house, and when you are walking by the way, and when you lie down, and when you rise.

Deuteronomy 31:12-13

Assemble the people, men, women, and little ones, and the sojourner within your towns, that they may hear and learn to fear the LORD your God, and be careful to do all the words of this law, and that their children, who have not known it, may hear and learn to fear the LORD your God, as long as you live in the land that you are going over the Jordan to possess.

> *Deuteronomy 32:45-46*
>
> *And when Moses had finished speaking all these words to all Israel, he said to them, "Take to heart all the words by which I am warning you today, that you may command them to your children, that they may be careful to do all the words of this law."*

These passages demonstrated the inter-generational concern that Moses advocated. He commanded the parents to *"make known"* (Deut. 4:9), *"teach"* (Deut. 6:7; 11:19), and *"command"* God's statutes to their children (Deut. 32:46). The goal is that the children may *"hear and learn to fear Yahweh"* (31:13). It is only when parents raise their children in the Word of God and take every opportunity to teach them that they too will come to know Yahweh and consequently live their lives for Him.

Moses not only cared about the Israelite households, he was also concerned about the community as a whole. We see, all along, he was exposing Joshua and training him to become the next generation leader. Joshua eventually became the new leader of the nation when Moses passed on. This was a daunting task and he was not unprepared for it.

JOSHUA

PREPARATION FOR LEADERSHIP

We learn about Joshua in the Book in the Bible named after him. There we read about how he successfully led the second generation of Israelites who came out of Egypt into the Promise Land. It is also in the Book of Joshua that we learn about his success in overcoming the inhabitants of the land and allocating the land to the different tribes of Israel. But we know of Joshua, even before that. In the Book of Exodus, we read that as soon as they crossed the Red Sea, they encountered the Amalekites. Joshua led the army to fight against and defeat them while Moses sat on an elevation and lifted up his hands in prayer. (Exod. 17) In this incident, Joshua learned the power of God and power of prayer. He recognized the connection between Moses' raising of hands in trust to God and his winning the battle. This is an important precept that he learned early in his training for leadership later on.

As they encamped on Mt. Sinai, Joshua accompanied Moses, Aaron, and the seventy elders on the mountain of God. There, he had a vision of God, worshiped God, and ate the meal prepared by God (Exod. 24:13). Joshua encountered firsthand the glory, power and holiness of God. This was reinforced by the great amount of time that he spent outside the tent of meeting as Moses' assistant. (Exod. 33:11)

When Moses was at the mountain when the people below were making the golden calf idol, Joshua was with Moses and heard the sound of the people worshipping the idol from there. (Exod. 32:17) He witnessed how Moses got angry and dealt with the people. Joshua learned the importance of true worship and loyalty to Yahweh, the one true God.

In the Book of Numbers, Joshua also stood out as an assistant of Moses. In Numbers 11:28 Joshua expresses concern for the elders prophesying in the camp.

At a crucial point in their journey into the Promise Land, Joshua served as one of the twelve spies sent into the land. (Num. 13) He and Caleb together, against the ten (10) other spies were a minority in urging Israel to go into the land (14:6, 30, 38; 26:6; 32:12; 34:16). The refusal of Israel to listen to them turned into a sad story which ended in that generation dying in the wilderness, and only Joshua, Caleb and the second-generation Israelites were able to enter the Promise Land.

Also in Numbers 13, Moses changed Joshua's name from Hoshea to Yehoshua. This is symbolic since Joshua ends up playing the role of a Savior for Israel. Hence, Joshua's role is considered as a type of Christ.

After God told Moses he would not enter the land, God also instructed Moses to set Joshua apart. Joshua was characterized as having the Spirit in him, a characteristic important in his leading Israel into the Promise Land. (Num. 27:18) Moses and the priests acknowledge his new role by the laying of hands on Joshua. (Num. 27:22-23)

Moses prepared Joshua and acknowledged him as the new leader who would take his place. (Deut. 1:38; 3:21; 3:28; 31:1–8) Three times, he admonished Joshua to "be strong and courageous" (Deut. 6, 7, 23). This admonition will be repeated three times at the beginning of Joshua's term. (Josh. 1)

From these episodes, we learn that Joshua did not suddenly become the new leader. He was prepared through the roles he was given while serving as the assistant of Moses. Aside from Moses, there were others who helped shape him to become a leader. Included are the religious leaders, the priest who acknowledged and supported him by the laying of hands; the military men who followed his commands in time of engagement against the enemies; other leaders, like Caleb, who shared his values and strong belief in Yahweh. These were instrumental in preparing and shaping Joshua to become the leader he came to be. As a result of these multiple influences, he was equipped and empowered to lead in the place of a great leader, Moses. When it was time for him to take on the leadership in the place of Moses, Joshua was well-prepared for the role. It was a daunting mission and he needed a lot of encouragement, yet he did not cower in fear but led Israel to successfully overcome their enemies and occupy the land. Beyond the military victory, Joshua was a great spiritual leader. He led the nation to commit to serve Yahweh faithfully. And this commitment, he demonstrated through his own family. His famous words, "As for me and my house, we will serve the Lord," still rings powerfully even in our time.

CALEB

THE BEGINNINGS

We do not know much about Caleb's early life, but we do know that he was about 40 years old when he was sent out to spy out the Promised Land, that was about 2 years after the Exodus. So, we could surmise that he was part of the group of Hebrews that exited Egypt during the Exodus. We could also surmise that Caleb was born and raised in Egypt. He grew up in that environment where they were working as slaves for the Egyptians. He was an adult when they left Egypt so he would already have vivid memories of the harsh conditions of life in Egypt. He would also have had well-developed faith convictions by the time of the Exodus and during the Sending of the Spies event. We know that Caleb had strong faith convictions because he demonstrated it during the *Spy Story in the Israelites journey*. He demonstrated what it means to fully trust the Lord and wholeheartedly obey him. Since Caleb was mature, yet young and strong enough, being 40 years old, he was chosen and recognized to lead the tribe of Judah, largest of the twelve tribes, along with other chosen leaders of their respective tribes. He was chosen to represent the tribe of Judah to spy out the land before they entered it.

> *"Send some men to explore the land of Canaan, which I am giving to the Israelites. From each ancestral tribe send one of its leaders." (Num. 13:2)*

Being one of the 12 spies, Caleb had the opportunity to do a reconnaissance of Canaan. They went along the ridge of the mountains from Hebron in the south to Rehob in the north. In this reconnaissance, they were to carefully note what they saw, including the fortifications of the cities, the produce of the land, and the kind of people who lived there.

In this exploration of the land, the city of Hebron made a mark on them, especially Caleb. We know because Caleb will later claim it as his allocation, as recorded in Joshua 14. Hebron[7] was a strong and fortified city strategically elevated on a hill, and its inhabitants were giants who descended from Anak. It was because of them that the 10 other spies were afraid to enter the land. These 10 other spies caused the whole community to be fearful and rebel.

"The people who live there are powerful, and the cities are fortified and very large. We even saw descendants of Anak there. We seemed like grasshoppers in our own eyes, and we looked the same to them." (Num. 13:28, 33) It was in the context of fear, hostility and unbelief that Caleb, and also Joshua, stood firm in courage and faith.

"Then Caleb silenced the people before Moses and said, 'We should go up and take possession of the land, for we can certainly do it." (Num. 13:30)

They tried hard to persuade the people to go in faith despite the daunting challenges they were faced with.

"The land we passed through and explored is exceedingly good. If the LORD (Yahweh) is pleased with us, he will lead us into that land, a land flowing with milk and honey, and will give it to us. Only do not rebel against the LORD. And do not be afraid of the people of the land, because we will swallow them up. Their protection is gone, but the LORD is with us. Do not be afraid of them." (Num. 14:7-9)

They had a strong belief that Yahweh was with them and would give them victory. They had faith that the Lord would keep His promise and enable them to conquer the land. In the end, they were not able to persuade the people who chose not to believe and to remain in fear.

---

7 Hebron is an ancient city, built seven years prior to Zoan in Egypt, and so could be dated to about 1700 BC.

But for their courage and their faith, Caleb and Joshua were the only ones from their generation who were able to enter the Promise Land.

CALEB KEPT THE FAITH UNTIL HIS OLD AGE

In his old age, Caleb was recognized as the outstanding spy-leader from the tribe of Judah 45 years previous. As the representative of the tribe of Judah, he addressed his old comrade, Joshua, recalled their story as spies, and reminded him of the inheritance assigned to him at that time by Moses.

> *"6 Now the men of Judah approached Joshua at Gilgal, and Caleb son of Jephunneh the Kenizzite said to him, 'You know what the LORD said to Moses the man of God at Kadesh Barnea about you and me. 7 I was forty years old when Moses the servant of the LORD sent me from Kadesh Barnea to explore the land. And I brought him back a report according to my convictions, 8 but my brothers who went up with me made the hearts of the people melt with fear. I, however, followed the LORD my God wholeheartedly. 9 So on that day Moses swore to me, 'The land on which your feet have walked will be your inheritance and that of your children forever, because you have followed the LORD my God wholeheartedly.'" (14:6-9)*

Before the land was allocated to the tribes, Caleb staked his claim over Hebron, which was promised to him by Moses then. *"Give Me This Mountain"* (Josh. 14:12)

Caleb's faith was fully demonstrated in Joshua 14:10-12.

> *"Just as the LORD promised, he has kept me alive for forty-five years ... so here I am today, eighty-five years old!" (14:10a)*

"I am still as strong today as the day Moses sent me out; I'm just as vigorous to go out to battle now as I was then." (14:11) "Now give me this hill country that the LORD promised me that day." (14:12a) "You yourself heard then that the Anakites were there and their cities were large and fortified, but the LORD helping me, I will drive them out just as he said." (14:12b)

Caleb had exercised his faith when he was young. He continued to exercise his faith when he became old. He acknowledged the promises of Yahweh, and recognized that it was Yahweh who helped all along, in standing up against opposition, in battling with their enemies and overcoming them.

As expected, Joshua granted Caleb's request, and gave him the whole hill country of Hebron. (Josh. 14:13-19; 15:15, 49). Apparently, the grant includes the city of Debir (Josh. 15:13-19), also known as Kiriath-Sepher (Josh. 15:15; Judg. 1:11) and Kiriath Sannah (Josh. 15:49).

"Then Joshua blessed Caleb son of Jephunneh and gave him Hebron as his inheritance. 14 So Hebron has belonged to Caleb son of Jephunneh, the Kenizzite ever since, because he followed the LORD, the God of Israel, wholeheartedly. 15 (Hebron used to be called Kiriath Arba after Arba, who was the greatest man among the Anakites.) Then the land had rest from war." (Josh. 14:13-15)

CALEB PASSED ON HIS FAITH TO HIS DAUGHTER

Caleb's daughter Acsah, took after her father's boldness and faith. In Joshua 15, she tells her husband to ask for a field from her father. "17 And Othniel the son of Kenaz, the brother of Caleb, captured it. And he gave him Acsah his daughter as wife. 18 When she came to him, she urged him to ask her father for a field. And she got off her donkey, and Caleb said to her, 'What do you want?' 19 She said to him, 'Give me a blessing. Since you have given me the land of the Negev, give me also springs of water.' And he gave her the upper springs and the lower springs." (15:17-19) But, even before her husband was able to do so, she found an opportunity to request it herself from her father.

"She replied, 'Do me a special favor. Since you have given me land in the Negev [desert], give me also the springs of water.' So Caleb gave her the upper and lower springs." (Josh. 15:19)

Since what she asked for an arid piece of land, she also asked for two water sources, the upper springs and the lower springs.[8] These must refer to water sources outside the natural territorial limits of Debir, but close enough to be transferred to its jurisdiction.

Acsah was straightforward in asking for what she wanted from her father, and Caleb granted it to her without hesitation. The dynamic was similar to how it was when he transacted with Joshua. Acsah's boldness showed her confidence in her father, which was also an example of faith. She was not afraid to ask for what she knew she needed, and her father willingly gave it to her.

FINAL THOUGHTS

THE CHALLENGING MISSION

The task of fulfilling God's mission is challenging. The path is not carved out, and there are a lot of obstacles to deal with.

One of the main hurdles in the fulfillment of God's call to Moses is Moses' own sense of inadequacy. He gave excuses for why he is not

---

[8] The word translated "springs" is *gullōṯ*, literally "basin(s)," defined by W. F. Albright as "subterranean pockets and basins of water under some of the wadis," to which access was gained by cutting a well shaft through the rock in the dry creek beds. Cf. Marten Woudstra, *The Book of Joshua*, The New International Commentary on the Old Testament. Grand Rapids, Michigan: Eerdmans, 1981, p. 242

cut for the job. Another hurdle is the lack of trust and support from Moses' own people. There was also powerful opposition Moses had to reckon with. Pharaoh was a powerful and ruthless person. He was considered a god in Egypt, and that he was unbeatable. That is why he was not threatened by the fact that Moses came in the name of Yahweh. He thought Yahweh was just the god of one tribal people. While he had a pantheon of gods on his side. Pharaoh could also muster all the forces and resources of Egypt to overcome the Israelites. The Israelites had no will, resources, training nor military might. And so, in Pharaoh's eyes, Moses and the Israelites could be disposed with a flick of a finger.

Joshua and Caleb had to do actual combat to overcome their enemies. This was tough considering how little preparation, experience and training they had for such encounters. Both of them also had to overcome the fear of the giants. Such fear was so great that the rest of the nation lost the privilege to enter the Promise Land. Yet, they had overcome their fears and emerged victorious in the end. They also faced great opposition from their own comrades and their own people. During the Spy Story, they were outnumbered, 2 to 10. They did not concede to the strong persuasive position of the majority because they firmly stood on the promises of God.

GOD'S EMPOWERMENT

Though the task may be challenging, God is with His servant and empowers them to do what God has called them to do.

God not only calls and leads, He accompanies His servants towards fulfilling the mission. God also provides concrete manifestations of His power and glory that support the mission of His servants. We see this in His powerful signs He gave to Moses, in the victories He gave to Joshua, and in the faithful support He gave to Caleb.

INTERGENERATIONAL AND MULTI-CULTURAL INFLUENCE AND COLLABORATION

We can see the impact of the older generation on the younger generation. And we can also see the importance of intergenerational collaboration in the fulfillment of the mission of God.

All of these three leaders were nurtured by their parents and parent-figures in their lives. And all three of them, in turn, influenced the generation coming after them.

While it is important for children to grow up independent, making their own choices, and owning their commitments, they have to be guided by the older, wiser, more experienced adults. This cannot be over-emphasized when it comes to faith convictions. It is the responsibility of older people to teach the truths of their beliefs to the next generation. While the younger generation will have to make their own decision about faith, they need to have the most valuable input from the adults in their lives. Otherwise, the inputs that will influence their choices will come from elsewhere.

We can also see among these leaders, inter-generational collaboration. Between Moses and Joshua, this is vividly portrayed at the battle against the Amalekites (Exod. 17:8-16). While Moses held up his hands, two men helped him hold it up, and Joshua was in the field battling the enemy. Moses stood on the hill with the staff of God in his hand, and Joshua overcame the Amalekites with a sword.

Moses could not have done the leading of Israelites out of Egypt towards the Promise Land without the younger generation of leaders helping him. Caleb and Joshua, for instance, was a generation younger than Moses when they spied out the land. Moses utilized their youthful strength and wisdom in accomplishing the mission.

Aside from intergenerational impact, we can also see multi-cultural or global forces at work in the shaping of the lives of these three leaders. They were exposed to other cultural values in their growing up years, and even at the height of their leadership. These influences provided either a contrast or a reinforcement to the familial values they received. Having a solid faith foundation, these leaders did not turn to the left or to the right, but stood on their firmly-held beliefs. In an environment where other cultural influences are competing with one's faith convictions, it is all the more imperative to underscore the importance of laying a strong faith foundation upon the next generation.

Yet, at the same time, some of these cultural influences can also be employed to enhance knowledge and contribute to the growth of the leader. Moses received instruction and training from his adoptive Egyptian family. He also gained valuable wisdom from a Midianite father-in-law. Caleb was a Kennite, a tribe that was not one of the 12 tribes of Israel. Yet, we know that he was absorbed into the tribe of Judah and even became a leader of the tribe.

Hence, we see that the development of individuals and their preparation to pursue their God-given mission involves not only a personal response, but the encouragement and providing of opportunities from experienced and more mature leaders to empower them to emerge as leaders. Moreover, it is not always a unidirectional effort from older leaders to younger ones. Sometimes, if not often times, it is a dynamic of working hand-in-hand and the accepting of each other's strength and gifts that results in a more effective accomplishment of the mission God has called them to.

An Intergenerational Partnership; the Story of Ruth and Naomi

Barbara Deutschmann

> "Where you go, I will go; where you lodge, I will lodge; your people shall be my people, and your God my God."

These words, spoken one to another, signal commitment, faithfulness, and love. So moving are they, that they are sometimes borrowed for wedding vows and for other occasions where unwavering public commitment is expressed.

Surprisingly, the Bible uses them of one woman to another. These women are unalike: the speaker, Ruth, is young, and the hearer, Naomi, is of an older generation. Ruth is a foreigner and Naomi, an Israelite about to return to her roots. In only one way are they alike: they are both now childless widows with an unknown future bound together in kinship and womanly solidarity.

The commitment of the younger to the older carries risk. Naomi shows signs of trauma. She has changed her name to 'Mara', bitter one, to express her sense of desolation and disappointment with God. She is rêqā, empty, hollowed out, by her grief (1:21). She sends the blame home to God as the one who has brought calamity on her.

This intergenerational partnership of the two women is an unusual one in the Bible. It was not missional in ways that involve going out and seeking others. It was missional in a way that we often see in the Old Testament in that it involved an ingrafting of a foreigner (Zech 8:23). Israel was meant to show by its life together, the character of their God, YHWH, and in so doing, attract others to their faith. The partnership of Naomi and Ruth shows the way that Israel's community, whilst very concerned to maintain its boundaries, in its best forms created space for and attracted the other.

In this chapter I will discuss women's vulnerabilities during the time in which the story is set, Iron-Age Israel, then highlight the plan of Naomi and Ruth to establish security for themselves. I will show how the Torah (law) of Israel created a structure of care but needed the women themselves to prod men into action. The conclusion will sum up the mission implications of the story.

TWO VULNERABLE WOMEN

Widows were a most vulnerable sub-group in ancient Israel. While a widow could inherit property in other ancient Near-Eastern states, in Israel she could not. Land allocations were small and based on a family's ability to manage it for their own livelihood.[9] Without men to do the work, a widow risked poverty (1 Kgs 17:12; Isa 54:4). When her husband died, a woman's options were to return to her father or live by charity (Deut 10:18; Ps 68:5–6).

The story of Ruth is familiar to Bible readers. The backdrop to the tale is severe drought. There was famine in the area of Bethlehem, the "house of bread" and a certain man took his wife and two sons to Moab, east of the Dead Sea (Ruth 1:1–2). Whilst in Moab, the

---

9 André LaCocque, Ruth: A Continental Commentary (Philadelphia, PA: Fortress Press, 2004), 22. Laura E. Donaldson, "The Sign of Orpah: Reading Ruth through Native Eyes," in Ruth and Esther, ed. Athalya Brenner (Sheffield: Sheffield Academic Press, 1999).

two sons marry Moabite women. The patriarch, Elimelech dies, and later, his two sons also die, leaving three widowed, childless women behind (1:4–5). Naomi sets off for Bethlehem where the famine has ended. One of her daughters-in-law, Orpah, does the more expected thing and returns to her mother's house (1:14–15).[10] Ruth, on the other hand, takes a leap into the unknown, committing herself to her mother-in-law, to Naomi's culture and importantly, to the Israelite God.

The story sounds familiar to those who follow world news. As I write, about 100 million people are displaced and, according to the United Nations High Commission for Refugees, about half of these are women.[11] Like Ruth and Naomi, these women are vulnerable to sexual violence, discrimination, and poverty.

What can we learn from the book of Ruth about intergenerational solidarity that confronts these problems?

Although often painted and presented as a rural idyll, the biblical story of Ruth has a harsh background. The women arrived in Jerusalem as the famine ends and the barley harvest is beginning. The staple starch for ancient Israel was bread and for the typical Israelite, grain-based food would have made up over half of their caloric intake.[12] Barley is the poor person's grain. It requires less water to grow so does a little better on marginal land. Across the Middle East, it is the bread of the poor.

Naomi and Ruth face a personal food crisis. Even supposing that they can get Elimelech's land into production, they will have over a year to wait. Their only choice is to glean. Gleaning in a barley harvest will declare them poor, as much as standing in a soup-kitchen line or rummaging in a dumpster might do today. Ruth's work as a gleaner will be fraught with danger of harassment from men in the field (2:9),

---

10 Laura E. Donaldson, "The Sign of Orpah: Reading Ruth through Native Eyes," in *Ruth and Esther*, ed. Athalya Brenner (Sheffield: Sheffield Academic Press, 1999).
11 https://www.unhcr.org/what-we-do/how-we-work/safeguarding-individuals/women
12 Jennifer L. Koosed, *Gleaning Ruth: A Biblical Heroine and Her Afterlives* (Columbia, S.C.: University of South Carolina Press, 2011), 64.

she will be anxious about whether she can get enough to eat, her back will ache, her skin will darken, and her hands will become calloused and crack.[13] Her hard work is met by the kindness of Boaz, who arranges for her safety and gives her food and drink (2:14).

SEEKING SECURITY

Naomi knows, however, that gleaning is only a temporary solution. Charity has its place, but it is no solution for vulnerable women. She seeks for Ruth's *manoaḥ*, security, a resting place, acceptance within the community of Bethlehem and the people of YHWH (3:1). When Boaz first meets Ruth, the Moabite, he expresses this wish for her with an image of refuge under the *kenap*, (wings) of YHWH, the God of Israel (2:12). Like a bird cossetting her chicks under expansive wings, Boaz avows that God offers refuge to Ruth, the Moabite gleaner.

Naomi and Ruth develop a plan to make this refuge a reality. The scheme strikes the reader as strange, bold, and risky. Much interpretative energy has gone into trying to understand this plan.[14] Ruth, washed, anointed, and dressed in her best, is to lay next to Boaz in his post-harvest sleep and when he stirs, do as he says. This is a risky and provocative challenge to him and seems to be the enactment of a marriage. Ruth cooperates fully with her mother-in-law's plan. On the threshing-floor, dressed in her finery, she asks Boaz to spread his *kenap* (wings) over her. In the early morning, she leaves the threshing-floor having secured Boaz's promise to act, with her apron full of grain, a symbol of future fertility.

This is a daring plan of two women whose options were few to secure their future. It gives the reader great insight into the precarious choices that women are often forced to make. Ruth was at great personal risk. Remember that men could have sex with unmarried

---

13 Koosed, Gleaning, 68–69.
14 Koosed, Gleaning, 90–93; Tikva S. Frymer-Kensky, Reading the Women of the Bible: A New Interpretation of Their Stories (New York, N.Y.: Schocken, 2002).

women without breaking any biblical law.[15] As long as she was not married or promised to another, and that she was not forced, young women were allowable sexual contacts. Naomi was counting on Boaz' character to act honourably and to understand the meaning of their ruse.

There was something else behind her plan. Naomi was counting on the operation of Torah regulations for community care. The Israelite law provided for a *go'el*, kinsman-redeemer to bear sons for a deceased brother by marrying and impregnating the brother's widow (Deut 25:510).[16] Boaz is not Mahlon's brother but Ruth's plea to Boaz in their threshing-floor encounter explicitly invokes this term and all that it involves (3:9) and Boaz recognizes this in his response (3:12–13). It seems that some mechanism of family responsibility was in place in Bethlehem at that time (Num 27:5–11). Boaz rises to the challenge and decides to act to provide for them. The bold plan of Naomi and Ruth recalled Boaz to his responsibilities under Israelite law.

The final chapter of the book neatly wraps up the story in a satisfying way. Boaz establishes that he is the closest kinsman to the women and takes Ruth, the Moabite as wife. This is remarkable because of her foreign status. According to Genesis 19, Moabites were the descendants of one of the two sons born to Lot after incestuous relations with his daughters when he was in a drunken state. Moab, the name of one of these sons, means "of the father," pointing to the incestuous origin of this people group. The laws of Deuteronomy repeat the negative assessment of Moabites, saying: "No Ammonite or Moabite shall enter the assembly of the Lord. Even to the tenth generation none of their descendants shall enter into the assembly of the Lord because they did not meet you with bread and water on your way out of Egypt" (Deut 23:3–6). The Moabites did not provide bread and water to the Israelites but they had provided hospitality

---

15 David M. Carr, The Erotic Word: Sexuality, Spirituality and the Bible (Oxford: Oxford University Press, 2003), 49–56. 8
16 Dvora E. Weisberg, "The Widow of Our Discontent: Levirate Marriage in the Bible and Ancient Isreal," Journal for the Study of the Old Testament 28, no. 4 (2004): 403–29.

to the family of Elimelech during the period of the famine. Boaz, perhaps in recognition, provides Ruth with bread and wine as she gleaned in his field (2:14).

This narrative shows how laws of the Torah were modified as they hit the real earth of a rural Israelite community. The law of the kinsman-redeemer was modified to become a responsibility to care for the vulnerable widow. The rigid exclusion of peoples such as Moabites, was softened to invite inclusion and respect.

Not only did Boaz do the right thing by Ruth, the community was also ready to embrace her. It is the women of the community who name what is happening to Naomi. They voice the significance of what has happened and situate it within the purposes of God for Israel: "Then the women said to Naomi, 'Blessed be YHWH who has not left you this day without next-of-kin; and may his name be renowned in Israel. He shall be to you a restorer of life and a nourisher of your old age'". The child born to Ruth and Boaz is seen as Naomi's. "Naomi took the child and laid him in her bosom and became his nurse. The women of the neighborhood gave him a name, saying, 'A son has been born to Naomi.' They named him Obed; he became the father of Jesse, the father of David" (4:14–17). The child is named and adopted by the whole community.

CONCLUSION

Like many biblical women, Ruth had an afterlife. She became the great-grandmother of Israel's king David, the monarch with metaphorical and physical links through to Joseph, father of Jesus (Matt 1). The book of Ruth makes much of this and links her to Rachel and Leah, whose children led to the twelve tribes of Israel. Ruth is linked to these matriarchs, most of whom were initially infertile and through direct intervention of God at the right time, gave birth to sons (Gen 29:31–35; 30:22–23).

This story of great-grandmother Ruth must have been told to king David. Did it influence his views of women? His views of YHWH? His sense of his role as protector of the weak and of the alien? Certainly, his relationships with women showed evidence of abuse. But there is a small hint that he carried the story of great-grandmother with him in the same way that family stories get carried down through generations. Do you remember that we noted what Boaz said to Ruth "May the Lord reward you . . . under whose wings you have come for refuge"? Ruth also used the same idea when, on the threshing floor, she asked Boaz to spread his wing over her. The only other place in the Old Testament where that phrase, under the wings of YHWH, occurs is in some psalms that are specifically linked to David (Ps 17, 36, 57, 61, 63, 91). We cannot be certain that David himself authored many of the psalms; they may have simply been attributed to him but the wings of YHWH is an image unique to Psalms and Ruth.

Another strand in Ruth's afterlife is in Matthew's genealogy in the New Testament. Ruth is one of five very unorthodox women mentioned in Jesus' family line, along with Tamar, Rahab, Bathsheba and Mary (Matt 1:1–16). These uncertain women model what Matthew calls the greater righteousness (Matt 5:43–48). Except for Mary, they are all foreigners with irregularity in their sexual lives yet each modelled *hesed*, that loving kindness which expressed God's character. In Matthew's reading of the Old Testament texts, righteousness is not found in Torah, a dry obedience as practiced by the pharisees and scribes of his day, but by common people, including women, who met calamity with a practical faith, stretching the boundaries of law and respectability to find new meanings to faith in God.

The intergenerational partnership of Ruth and Naomi withstood many perils to find *manoah*, a resting place, under God's wings. The mission that we see in action in their story is that of inclusion, the softening of boundaries to include others formerly seen as enemies. It merges "them" and "us", "sender" and "recipient" into a common humanity. Both the Moabite and the Israelite women were in need of each other and in need of God's care. It is mission to those brought close to us by their need. It is mission in solidarity with the refugee, the widow and orphan in recognition that we are all in need of a place under God's wings.

BIBLIOGRAPHY

Carr, David M. The Erotic Word: Sexuality, Spirituality and the Bible. Oxford: Oxford University Press, 2003.

Donaldson, Laura E. "The Sign of Orpah: Reading Ruth through Native Eyes." In Ruth and Esther, edited by Athalya Brenner, 130–44. Sheffield: Sheffield Academic Press, 1999.

Frymer-Kensky, Tikva S. Reading the Women of the Bible: A New Interpretation of Their Stories. New York, N.Y.: Schocken, 2002.

Koosed, Jennifer L. Gleaning Ruth: A Biblical Heroine and Her Afterlives. Columbia, S.C.: University of South Carolina Press, 2011.

LaCocque, André. Ruth: A Continental Commentary. Philadelphia, PA: Fortress Press, 2004. Weisberg, Dvora E. "The Widow of Our Discontent: Levirate Marriage in the Bible and Ancient Israel." Journal for the Study of the Old Testament 28, no. 4 (06// 2004): 40329.

Intergenerational Mission in the New Testament: Examples of Life-on-Life Modeling by Jesus and Paul

Narry F. Santos

INTRODUCTION

Intergenerational mission requires faith formation and leadership transmission that offer "a life-on-life encounter. . . (and) an investment of all that you are in another person."[17] Without a life-on-life encounter, intergenerational mission degenerates into a mere transfer of teaching and skill. As a leader, our task of forming and transmitting our life to another begins with biblical modeling.

---

17 Keith Phillips, *The Making of a Disciple* (New Jersey: Fleming Revell, 1975), 15.

This chapter seeks to unpack this kind of modeling in the New Testament from the life-changing examples of Jesus toward his disciples and of Paul toward Timothy, and from the commands of Paul to the Corinthian and Philippians churches to imitate him and what he does. We will see how their examples and commands show a "consistent manifestation of the message embodied in an attractive, visible lifestyle."[18]

As used in this chapter, modeling refers to the method in the intergenerational mission process that employs "transmission by example."[19] In this method, the biblical models by Jesus and Paul equip the next-generation leaders through examples that come out of the character and lifestyle of Jesus and Paul. Such modeling results in the imitation by emerging leaders (Jesus' disciples, Timothy, and church leaders), so that their imitation's "outcome is to shift the action from the model to the imitator."[20] Thus, imitation becomes part of the central process in the growth and transformation of the upcoming leaders toward inter-generational mission.

BRIEF STUDY OF THE NEW TESTAMENT TERMS FOR "MODEL"

The New Testament is colored with four different words that paint the varied shades of meaning for modeling. These four words are *tupos* (example), *hupodeigma* (copy), *summimatas* (fellow imitator), and *acholootheo* (to follow after) along with *paracholootheo* (to follow closely).

---

18 Chong Hiok Chan, "A Study on the Essential Nature of Role Modelling for the Effective Communication" (Thesis, University of the Philippines College of Baguio), 5.
19 Leroy Eims, *The Lost Art of Disciple Making* (Grand Rapids: Zondervan, 1978), 98.
20 Barbara M. Newman and Philip Newman, *Development through Life: A Psychological Approach* (Chicago: Dorsey, 1987), 222.

TUPOS: EXAMPLE FOR EXEMPLARY CONDUCT

The word *tupos* occurs sixteen times in the New Testament. Technically, the word "example" means "model or pattern."[21] It is the visible impression of a stroke, pressure, mark, or trace. The word historically comes from a strengthened Greek verb to "thump, cudgel, or pummel with a stick,"[22] projecting the picture of causing an imprint due to repeated blows.

Figuratively, "example" signifies a style or resemblance specifically designed as a model for imitation or instance of warning. Morally speaking, the word connotes being a pattern for exemplary moral conduct (1 Thess. 1:7; 1 Tim. 4:12; Titus 2:7; 1 Pet. 5:3). It is being a model in thought, word, and action so that others can follow the exemplary model in their own thoughts, words, and actions.

HUPODEIGMA: COPY THAT REFLECTS THE ORIGINAL

The word *hupodeigma* (copy) has the sense of a "document, proof, or even model."[23] In a different context, the same word may also mean "an exhibit for imitation and warning."[24] "Copy" also suggests the use of an image denoting what is similar (Heb. 8:6; 9:23ff). Thus, the picture of an original object may be seen as reflecting it, and therefore as a copy, or as indicating what is seen in the spirit, and therefore as a representative or model.[25]

---

[21] William F. Arndt and Wilbur Gingrich, *A Greek-English Lexicon of the New Testament and Other Early Christian Literature* (Chicago: University of Chicago Press, 1952), 837.
[22] James Strong, *A Concise Dictionary of the Words in Greek New Testament* (Nashville: Abingdon, 1975), 74.
[23] Schlier, "Copy." Gerhard Kittel, Gerhard Friedrich, and Geoffrey W. Bromily (Grand Rapids: Eerdmans, 1878), 33.
[24] Strong, *Concise Dictionary in Greek*, 105.
[25] Schlier, "Copy," p. 33.

SUMMIMATAS: IMITATION BY SIMILARITY, RECOGNITION OF AUTHORITY, AND OBEDIENCE

In the New Testament, the word group of *summimatas* (imitation) is represented by the word *mimeomai* (imitate), which occurs four times, and *summimatas* (fellow imitator), which occurs only once in Philippians 3:17. These two words are used in three ways; namely: (1) imitation as simple comparison due to similarity (1 Thess. 2:14); (2) imitation as recognition of authority (2 Thess. 3:7, 9; Phil. 3:7); and (3) imitation as requirement for total obedience to authority (1 Cor. 11:1; 1 Thess. 1:6; Eph. 5:1).

ACHOLOOTHEO: TO FOLLOW A TEACHING OR PERSON

The words in this word group are *acholootheo* (to follow), which occurs fifty-four times, and *epacholootheo* (to follow after) and *paracholootheo* (to follow closely), both occurring four times each. Specifically, *acholootheo* means to follow with respect, as servants would have for their master, and in the case of Jesus Christ, as the twelve apostles did in discipleship and fellowship (Matt. 8:22; Luke 9:6). *Epacholootheo* means to follow after the cause of God, and *paracholootheo* refers to following a teaching closely (Luke 1:3).

BIBLICAL MODELING EXAMPLES OF JESUS AND PAUL

Having seen the four different words for model, let us now proceed to the modeling relationships of Jesus with his disciples and of Paul with Timothy. Jesus and Paul exemplified lifestyles that made life-changing impact on the people they sought to love, serve, and lead.

JESUS' MODEL TO THE DISCIPLES

Jesus is the perfect Master Model worthy of full imitation. All areas of his life are areas that his disciples could emulate. For this study, I will simply discuss two of the traits that Jesus modeled throughout his life toward his disciples. These traits are prayer and obedience.

JESUS' MODEL OF PRAYERFULNESS

Prayer served as the bedrock of Jesus' ministry. "Every major event in His life was accompanied by prayer."[26] At his baptism, Jesus was found praying (Luke 3:21-22). Before he selected the twelve disciples, he spent an entire night in prayer: "One of those days Jesus went out to a mountainside to pray, and spent the night praying to God" (Luke 6:12, NIV). Just before sending out the Twelve, Jesus declared to them: "The harvest is plentiful but the workers are few. Ask the Lord of the harvest, therefore, to send out workers into his harvest field" (Matt. 9:37-38).

Jesus was praying when Peter testified that Jesus was the Christ (Luke 9:18-20). A week later, Jesus transfigured while he was praying (Luke 9:28-29). He also prayed for his disciples, rising long before daybreak to pray alone, apparently doing so every morning"[27] (Mark 1:35; Luke 4:42). His model of prayer had been so influential in the lives of the Twelve that while he was praying, they came to him and asked them to teach them to pray (Luke 11:1).

The life of Jesus was saturated with prayer. Even on his last day with the Twelve, he promised them the Holy Spirit, saying that he would pray to the Father, and the Father would send the Spirit to them (John 14:16; 16:7). In his high priestly prayer, Jesus prayed for his disciples (John 17). Again, at the garden of Gethsemane, he prayed and signified submission to the Father's will (Matt. 26:36-44).

---

26 Carl Wilson, *With Christ in the School of Disciple Building* (Grand Rapids: Zondervan, 1979), 224.
27 Wilson, *With Christ*, 224.

Aside from showing the value of prayer by being the example of it, Jesus also instructed his disciples to pray. He taught them the following principles on prayer: "But when you pray, go into your room, close the door and pray to your Father, who is unseen. Then your Father, who sees in secret, will reward you" (Matt. 6:6); "Ask and it will be given to you; seek and you will find; knock and the door will be opened to you" (Matt. 7:7); and "Watch and pray so that you will not fall into temptation" (Matt. 26:41a).

Jesus' teaching and modeling on prayer bore fruit in the lives of the disciples. They followed Jesus' example in praying. After the resurrection appearances of Jesus, they met to pray (Acts 2:42). Examples of prayer by the disciples confirmed that Jesus' influence on prayer had a positive effect on them. These examples include the following instances: when Peter and John went to the temple to pray (Acts 4:1); when the apostles appointed deacons to take care of the ministry of food distribution so that the apostles could devote their time to prayer and the ministry of the Word (Acts 6:1-4); and when Peter and John prayed and laid their hands on the Samaritan Christians, imparting the Holy Spirit to them (Acts 8). Without the model of Jesus's prayerfulness, the disciples could not have seen the priority of prayer in their own ministry. For them, praying became important because they saw prayerfulness in their Master's Model.

JESUS' MODEL OF OBEDIENCE

Another trait that Jesus modeled to his disciples was obedience to God's will. The following three verses attest to his absolute submission to his Father in the Gospel of John: (1) "for I seek not to please myself but him who sent me" (John 5:30b); (2) "For I have come down from heaven not to do my will but to do the will of him who sent me" (John 6:38a); and (3) "The one who sent me is with me; he has not left me alone; for I always do what pleases him" (John 8:29).

Jesus was obedient to the point of accomplishing all that the Father wanted him to do (John 6:36). In his high priestly prayer, Jesus said, "I have brought you glory on earth by finishing the work you gave me to do" (John 17:4). In the garden of Gethsemane, he totally surrendered his will: "Father, if you are willing, take this cup from me; yet not my will, but yours be done" (Luke 22:42). At the cross, Jesus was able to exclaim, "It is finished!" (John 19:30a), because he completed his mission of salvation on earth.

Additionally, Jesus taught obedience to his disciples. One of his most important sayings was "Whoever has ears, let them hear" (Matt. 11:15). The Hebraic meaning refers to the admonition for a person to have willing ears to give respectful attention and obedience to what God is saying. Jesus warned that the one who hears his words and does not put them into practice is like the foolish person who built their house on sand and is carried away when a flood comes (Matt. 7:26-27). But the wise person who hears the words of Jesus and puts them into practice is like a person who builds on a rock foundation that stands amid the storms of life (Matt. 7:24-25). Moreover, Jesus taught that the source of blessing in the Christian life is obedience (John 14:15-17, 21, 24; 15:10-12).

Jesus' teaching and model of obedience produced obedience in the disciples. Peter and John boldly testified before the Sanhedrin, "Which is right in God's eyes: to listen to you, or to him? You be the judges! As for us, we cannot help speaking about what we have seen and heard" (Acts 4:19-20). The two apostles obey God, not people. On another occasion, after being imprisoned and reprimanded for preaching in the name of Jesus, the apostles declared before the Council, "We must obey God rather than human beings!" (Acts 5:29).

Peter taught obedience in his epistle. He wrote in three instances: (1) "to be obedient to Jesus Christ" (1 Pet. 1:2b); (2) "As obedient children, do not conform to the evil desires you had when lived in ignorance" (1 Pet. 1:14); and (3) "you have purified yourselves by obeying the truth" (1 Pet. 1:22a). Peter was able to teach on obedience because he himself had to learn obedience to Jesus and his words. He obeyed Jesus' mandate to shepherd and tend his sheep (John 21:15-17). After shepherding the flock of God, Peter exhorted the elders of Asia Minor to do likewise. He gave this command to them: "Be shepherds of God's flock that is under your care" (1 Pet. 5:2a).

PAUL'S MODELING TO TIMOTHY

Aside from the modeling of Jesus towards the disciples, the modeling of Paul is also commendable. Paul has been described as a leader of God who "had the heart of a pastor, the mind of a scholar, the feet of a missionary, the drive of an evangelist, and the hide of an elephant!"[28] One significant contribution of Paul was his "reproduction" of another leader of God who had the heart of a pastor, the feet of a missionary, and the drive of an evangelist. He was able to "reproduce" these qualities in Timothy through his consistent modeling. What were the significant qualities that Paul modelled to Timothy? These qualities were concern for people and the sense of responsibility in the Lord's work. These qualities were crucial in the propagation of the ministry of God's servants.

PAUL'S MODEL OF CONCERN FOR PEOPLE

Paul abounded in his examples of concern for people. He showed concern for the converts in his ministry during the first missionary journey by going back to them. The goal for his return was to aid them in their growth in the Lord (Acts 15:36). He felt for his Galatian friends when they were being led astray from freedom back to spiritual bondage, saying: "My dear children, for whom I am again in the pains of childbirth until Christ is formed in you" (Gal. 4:19).

The range of Paul's warmth of affection was a quality that no attentive reader of his letters could miss. In the case of the Philippian believers, if a contribution was necessary to complete their faith in the form of a "drink offering on the sacrifice and service coming from your faith" (Phil. 2:17a), then the outpouring of Paul's life would be that drink offering. He was also willing to be "cursed and cut off from Christ, if only the salvation of his fellow Jews could be achieved" (Rom. 9:3).[29]

---

28 Jerry Falwell. *Champions for God* (Wheaton: Victor, 1985), 123.
29 F. F. Bruce, *Paul: Apostle of the Heart Set Free* (Grand Rapids: Eerdmans, 1984), 457.

For Paul, the people who turn over their lives to Jesus were his pride and joy. When he wrote to them, he was like a father addressing his own children. He commended them for their praiseworthy deeds and scolded them for their shortcomings. "He warns them that if they do not mend their ways, he would take a big stick with him next time he comes"[30] (cf. 1 Cor. 4:12). Thus, we can see that Paul's concern for people stopped at nothing less than seeking their best, whether his concern was expressed in commendation or rebuke.

Timothy caught Paul's concern for people and also practiced it in his lifetime. In fact, there is ample evidence that Paul wholeheartedly appreciated the selfless devotion with which Timothy supported and served him for the rest of his elderly life."[31] Paul highly spoke of Timothy when the former proposed to send the letter as Paul's representative to Philippi:

> *I hope in the Lord to send Timothy to you soon, that I also may be cheered when I receive news about you. I have no one else like him, who will show genuine concern for your welfare. For everyone looks out for their own interests, not those of Jesus Christ. But you know that Timothy has proved himself, because as a son with his father he has served with me in the work of the gospel. (Phil. 2:19-22)*

Timothy surrendered whatever personal ambitions he might have cherished in order to play the part of a son to Paul and to help him in his missionary activity. Timothy showed a selfless concern for others that matched the apostle's eagerness to spend and be spent for them.[32]

---

30 Bruce, *Paul*, 457.
31 H. C. Kee, "Timothy," in *Interpreter's Dictionary of the Bible* edited by George Arthur Buttrick (Nashville, Abingdon, 1962).
32 Herbert Lockyer, *All the Men of the Bible* (Grand Rapids: Zondervan, 1958), 329.

PAUL'S SENSE OF RESPONSIBILITY FOR THE LORD'S WORK

Along with his modeling of concern for people, Paul also showed a true sense of responsibility in the Lord's work. His life was consumed in fulfilling his call both to the Jews and Gentiles. He proclaimed the gospel anywhere he went, planted churches in strategic centers, and wrote letters of exhortation and teaching.

Paul was also so consumed in serving the Lord that he said, "However, I consider my life worth nothing to me; my only aim is to finish the race and complete the task the Lord Jesus has given me—the task of testifying to the good news of God's grace" (Acts 20:24). He also confidently asserted at the end of his ministry, "I have fought the good fight, I have finished the race, I have kept the faith" (2 Tim. 4:7). Paul was undoubtedly responsible in fulfilling his God-appointed task until the end of his life.

Like his spiritual father, Timothy excelled in responsible service to God. He became the trusted and faithful associate of Paul. He was also considered by Paul as a "fellow-worker" (Rom. 16:21), who served as a responsible emissary. In Philippians 2:19, he was dispatched by Paul to bring an eyewitness report of the state of the Philippian church. Later in Timothy's ministry, he was sent from Ephesus to Macedonia, along with Epaphras (Acts 19:22). Timothy was entrusted with more responsibility as Paul saw his stable sense of responsibility being displayed in their continued ministry together.

Having been ordained as minister of the gospel (1 Tim. 4:14; 2 Tim. 1:6-7), Timothy became an ambassador charged with difficult tasks. He responsibly handled the delicate mission of restoring the backsliding Corinthian church and of giving comfort to the persecution-stricken Thessalonian church. Lastly, he was a co-sufferer with Paul in the afflictions of the gospel (2 Tim. 1:8). Tradition states that Timothy died, like his mentor, as a martyr for his faithfulness and sense of responsibility as bishop in the reign of Domitian or Nerva.

In summary, Timothy exhibited the same sense of responsibility that Paul modeled to him. This modeling of the qualities of concern and responsibility occurred because Timothy had a close and trusting relationship with Paul. Paul described Timothy as "my true son in the faith" (1 Tim. 1:2a). This closeness between Paul and Timothy made modeling more effective in their relationship and partnership.

PAUL'S COMMANDS TO IMITATE HIM AND WHAT HE DID

After having seen the modeling examples of Jesus to the disciples and of Paul to Timothy, we now discuss two instances in the New Testament when Paul commanded the Corinthian believers to imitate him and the Philippian Christians to imitate what he does. Paul's commands highlight the importance of imitating what has been intentionally modeled to the churches, so that they can also model the same examples to their next-generation leaders.

PAUL'S COMMAND FOR THE CORINTHIANS TO IMITATE HIM

In chapter four of 1 Corinthians, Paul warned the Corinthian believers of pride and conceit, so that "you will not be puffed up in being a follower of one of us over against the other" (1 Cor. 4:6). To ward off misunderstanding of his warning, Paul explained further: "I am not writing this to shame you but to warn you as my dear children" (1 Cor. 4:14). He was committed to build and encourage them, not to destroy and discourage them.

After establishing his rightful claim as spiritual father, Paul proceeded to exhort the Corinthians on modeling. He wrote, "Therefore I urge you to imitate me" (1 Cor. 4:16). The present form of the verb is graphic: "continue to become in practice (imitators)"[33] or "keep on becoming imitators of me."[34] In moral exhortations, the

---

33 W. H. Mare, "1 Corinthians" in *The Expositor's Bible Commentary* edited by Frank E. Gaebelein, vol. 10 (Grand Rapids: Zondervan, 1976), 216.
34 Archibald T. Robertson, *Word Pictures in the New Testament*, vol. 4 (Grand Rapids: Baker, 1931), 109.

verb communicated this thought: "be in effect and show yourselves"[35] as imitators of who I am. Imitating here demanded a display of a "character formed on the given model."[36] Paul was the given model from which the Corinthians should pattern from character.

In addition, the idea of Paul's exhortation on modeling communicated that imitation was the law of the children's life. Children "naturally imitate the actions and attitudes of their fathers and mothers."[37] In Paul's case, the Corinthian spiritual children were to naturally imitate the actions and attitudes of their spiritual father Paul. They could not accomplish such imitation by simply saying, "I am of Paul" (1 Cor. 1:12). They need to tread in Paul's steps.

Treading on Paul's steps would embrace, in effect, much of what struggling for the advance of the gospel entailed. Paul described this struggle for the gospel as a litany of seemingly humiliating situations (1 Cor. 4:9-13). These situations involved being tagged as persons condemned to death, as spectacles to the world, fools for Christ's sake, weak, without honor, hungry and thirsty, poorly clothed, roughly treated, and homeless (1 Cor. 4:9-11). Paul went on to explain how he and his companions, as ministers, responded to these seemingly humiliating conditions: "We work hard with our own hands. When we are cursed, we bless; when we are slandered, we answer kindly. We have become the scum of the earth, the garbage of the world—right up to this moment" (1 Cor. 4:12-13). Paul's intent in his exhortation was for the Corinthians to follow the entire practice of the ministry he modeled.[38]

It is worthwhile to know that the exhortation for the Corinthians to be followers of Paul was not ill-fitting in a context which warned against pride and conceit. There were two reasons for this. First, as an apostle, Paul was not simply teaching the Christian faith but was also showing the significance of it in everyday life.[39] He had to

---

35 W. Robertson Nicoll, *The Expositor's Greek Testament*, vol. 2 (Grand Rapids: Eerdmans, 1967), 804.
36 Nicoll, *Expositor's Greek Testament*, 804.
37 Mare, "1 Corinthians," 804.
38 F. W. Grosheide, *Commentary on the First Epistle to the Corinthians* (Grand Rapids: Eerdmans, 1980), 113.
39 Grosheide, *First Corinthians*, 113.

exhibit the content of his teaching being applied to the practical activities of daily living. Paul used his real-life activities as model and commanded them to do likewise. Second, since Paul was the spiritual father of the Corinthians, he had the right to expect that his example be followed.[40] He expected them to imitate his attitudes in facing his experiences as God's minister (1 Cor. 4:9-13). In Paul, the Corinthians saw examples of humility and selflessness, which would serve as the deterrent to pride and conceit.

Paul continued his exhortation on modeling by telling them that he has sent them Timothy, his beloved child in the Lord (1 Cor. 4:17). To his "dear children" (1 Cor. 4:14a), Paul sent "my son whom I love" (1 Cor. 4:17a). The beloved child's task was to help the Corinthians in their progress in imitating their spiritual father. He was to admonish them to keep on following Paul's example. Moreover, Timothy "will remind you of my way of life in Christ Jesus" (1 Cor. 4:17b). Timothy's reminding them implied that Paul had lived in Corinth, that everyone has seen his conduct, and had been familiar with his ways.

As Paul's "mirror-image," Timothy would also remind the Corinthians of Paul's teachings. He was best qualified to remind them because Paul personally modeled to him his teachings. So, Paul had confidence in Timothy in being able to teach his ways. "My ways" was a semitic expression signifying a person's conduct.[41] The phrase also meant habits of life to be copied, not just to be learned. These habits of life were those which are in Christ (1 Cor. 4:17c). This phrase showed that Paul's conduct was ruled by Christ, and only in so far as it was, could it be an example to the Corinthians.

Timothy would remind the Corinthians of Paul's ways in Christ, "which agrees with what I teach everywhere in every church" (1 Cor. 4:17d). These words were again used in reference to Paul's teachings and conduct, showing that doctrine and life always go together. Although the ways and teachings of Paul were not the same thing, the former were regulated by the latter. This again stressed the value of modeling in life and creed.

---

40 Grosheide, *First Corinthians*, 113.
41 Grosheide, *First Corinthians*, 114.

Because Timothy personally experienced Paul's modeling, he knew firsthand the consistency of ways and teachings that Paul exemplified. That is why Timothy could also teach the Corinthians what Paul taught everywhere, which was, that people imitate his conduct. In every church, Paul expected his ways and teachings to be followed. In the case of Corinth, Timothy was to make sure that the Corinthians obeyed Paul's exhortation.

In summary, the exhortation on modeling in Corinth was supported by the lifestyle of Paul that helped the Corinthians know how to imitate Paul. He had even proven the success of modeling in the person of Timothy. So, he commissioned Timothy to assist the Christians in following Paul's ways, which were in Christ. Thus, 1 Corinthians 4:14-17 teaches clearly that modeling works individually (for Timothy) and corporately (for the church in Corinth).

PAUL'S COMMAND FOR THE PHILIPPIANS TO IMITATE WHAT HE DID

In 1 Corinthians 4:14-17, Paul exhorted the Corinthian Christians to follow his model. In Philippians 4:9, Paul commanded the Philippian believers to do the same things he does. Before explaining this command, a brief summary of its context is necessary. Paul enumerated the proper subjects of reflection or meditation in Philippians 4:8. These subjects are as follows: "whatever is true, whatever is noble, whatever is right, whatever is admirable—if anything is excellent or praiseworthy, dwell on these things." (Phil. 4:8).

After listing these subjects of meditation, Paul proceeded to indicate the appropriate line of action, which was to put them into practice (Phil. 4:9b). The verb "practice" contains the idea of continuity and repetition, and the present tense calls for a continual practicing.[42] In addition to continual practicing, the command

---

42 Fritz Rienecker and Cleon Rogers, *Linguistic Key to the Greek New Testament* (Grand Rapids: Baker, 1980), 561.

involves the task of "marking activity in its progress."[43] Thus, to practice required not only regularity in frequency but also in the increase of the frequency's quantity and in the quality of the practice. Paul expected the Philippians to practice the qualities as a habit and with earnestness and perseverance.[44]

The question that needs to be addressed is this: "What were 'these things' that were to be practiced as a habit and with perseverance?" "These things" were "whatever you have learned or received or heard from me, or seen in me" (Phil. 4:9a). This verse naturally belonged to what preceded rather than to what followed. Thus, the structure of the sentence could be rendered as follows: "'Whatever things are true' and the rest—'if there be any virtue, and if there be any praise, think of these things—which you also learned, and received, and heard, and saw in me."[45]

It seems possible that the Philippians personally learned, received, heard, or saw in Paul all the subjects of meditation listed above. In fact, that could be the reason why Paul did not hesitate to command the Christians to practice them. The command was not totally new to the Philippians. Paul first taught and modeled the teachings to them when he was with them. It was as if the Philippians could hear Paul saying, "I showed through my life the moral principles I taught you and am now asking you to recall in your minds."

The four verbs in this verse should be connected in pairs.[46] The first, "learned and received," referred to what the Philippians had learned from Paul's teaching. The second pair, "heard and saw," alluded to what they had learned from his example.[47] Thus, they had to obey the apostle's precepts as indicated by "learned and received" and to follow his example as shown by "heard and saw."

---

[43] Marvin R. Vincent, *A Critical and Exegetical Commentary on the Epistles to the Philippians and Philemon* (New York: Charles Scribner's Sons, 1987), 140.

[44] Kenneth S. Wuest, *Philippians in the Greek New Testament* (Grand Rapids: Eerdmans, 1973), 111.

[45] Wuest, *Philippians*, 388.

[46] J. B. Lightfoot, *St. Paul's Epistle to the Philippians* (Grand Rapids: Zondervan, 1980), 162.

[47] Vincent, *Philippians and Philemon*, 140.

More specifically, the learning was done by personal instruction while the receiving was seen as oral epistolary traditions obtained by the Philippians from Paul or transmitted by his delegates.[48] The verbs "heard and saw" referred to the Philippians' personal contact with Paul. The difference between heard and saw was that the former referred to what the Philippians heard when Paul was absent, while the latter referred to the time when Paul was present in Philippi.

Whether the Philippians were present with or absent from Paul, they still learned from Paul or about Paul and his ministry. When with them, Paul personally instructed the believers both by precept and example. When not in their midst, he sent his emissaries or wrote letters to them. Thus, Paul could command the Philippians to practice the things they learned, received, heard, and saw in him because of his consistency in precept and example.

In summary, the two New Testament passages discussed above (1 Cor. 4:14-17 and Phil. 4:9) show the need and command to imitate Paul and his ministry. To the Corinthians, Paul gave the exhortation to be imitators of him. To the Philippians, he gave the command to habitually practice his teachings and imitate his examples. He was able to exhort and command them to imitate him because he demonstrated a lifestyle and ministry that were worthy of imitation.

LESSONS ON MODELING AND INTERGENERATIONAL MISSION FROM THE NEW TESTAMENT

This chapter has just reviewed the value of life-on-life modeling, as exemplified by Jesus and Paul, so that intergeneration mission can occur, especially as it relates to engaging and equipping the next-generation leaders, as experienced by Jesus' disciples, Timothy, and church leaders in Corinth and Philippi. We also saw the importance of imitation, as appropriate response in the central process of growth

---

48 Vincent, *Philippians and Philemon*, 140.

and transformation by upcoming leaders toward intergenerational mission.

From the brief survey on the different New Testament words for model, we learn the use of example or pattern for exemplary and model conduct (*tupos*), the use of copy or reflection of the original (*hupodeigma*), the importance of the response of imitation as simple comparison, recognition of a person's authority, or obedience to the command to imitate God (*summimatas and mimeotai*), and the needed actions to follow a respected person (*acholootheo*), to follow after the cause of God (*ephacholootheo*), and to carefully follow a teaching or doctrine (*paracholootheo*). These various nuances of life-on-life modeling highlight the need to become examples and to imitate exemplary models as a response. The lesson to be learned here is that we can be effective mentors for the next generation of leaders when we first become effective models in life, relationship, and ministry.

To see how life-on-life modeling occurs, we learn from the model of Jesus to his disciples in the areas of prayer and obedience and from the example of Paul to Timothy in the areas of concern for people and the sense of responsibility in the Lord's work. The exemplary examples of Jesus and Paul show that modeling is effective in embodying through their attractive, visible lifestyle the message of the gospel of God's grace and all of God's teaching. The lesson to be learned here is that intergenerational mission can flourish when models of character become ministers of care to others.

Finally, the two Pauline commands to the Corinthians ("I urge you to imitate me" [1 Cor. 4:16]) and to the Philippians ("whatever you have learned or received or heard from me, or seen in me—put it into practice" [Phil. 4:9]) teach us the important lesson of intentionality. Just as life-on-life modeling needs to be intentional, so the imitation of exemplary modeling must be intentional. For when modeling and imitation become intentional, then inter-generational mission never becomes accidental nor incidental.

II. Sociological, Anthropological, Theological, And Missiological Aspects of Intergenerational Mission

Engaging the Next Generation in God's Global Mission

Jolene Erlacher

"When you were born has a larger effect on your personality and attitudes than the family who raised you does."

–Dr. Jean Twenge

Young people today differ from older generations in significant ways. Globalization, migration, economic policies, media and the internet have, and continue to, erode cultural boundaries in unprecedented ways. The generations born into this period of accelerating change share experiences, values, attitudes, and behaviors with peers around the world. As a result, today's generational shifts are significant and profound, resulting in meaningful implications for families, societies, and ministry efforts globally.

GLOBAL YOUTH CULTURE

Historically, generational differences have existed in many cultures. Jean Twenge explained, "Generations aren't just an American phenomenon; most other countries have similar generational divisions, though with their own cultural twists."⁴⁹ Unlike the previous generations, however, who were more significantly impacted by their national and local cultures, young Millennials (b. 1981-1995), Generation Z (b. 1996-2010), and Generation Alpha (b. 2011-) are increasingly influenced by global trends. This has resulted in the emergence of a global youth culture. Steiger International, a worldwide youth ministry active in over 120 cities globally, indicated, "Today, young people all over the world are more similar than ever, making up a truly Global Youth Culture. The Global Youth Culture, ranging in age between 17 and 35, can be found in every major city on the planet."⁵⁰ Ben Pierce explained, "Secularization, a trend closely tied to the globalization of culture among urban youth, is not limited to post-Christian regions like Europe or the USA. It is impacting cultures in urban centers in every region of the world, including the Middle East, Asia, and Africa."⁵¹

So, what connects this generation? Globalization and technology are contributing to the transmission of ideas, values, and beliefs across borders. Many young people today have grown up in a world dominated by video games, pornography, and social media.⁵² As a result, this next generation, connected by secularism, consumerism, social media, and the entertainment industry, forms the largest global culture to ever exist.⁵³ As young people follow the same social media influencers, watch the same Tik Tok videos, listen to the same music, and interact with others who share their interests, their connection to peers in different parts of the world is sometimes stronger than

---

49 Jean Twenge, *Generations: The Real Differences Between Gen Z, Millennials, Gen X, Boomers, and Silents–and What They Mean for America's Future* (New York: Atria Books, 2023), 2.

50 "What Is the Global Youth Culture," Steiger, October 19, 2023, https://steiger.org/about-us/the-gyc.

51 Ben Pierce, "Connecting with the New Global Youth Culture," Lausanne Movement, August 31, 2023, https://lausanne.org/content/lga/2019-03/connecting-with-the-new-global-youth-culture.

52 "What Is the Global Youth Culture," Steiger, October 19, 2023, https://steiger.org/about-us/the-gyc.

53 Ben Pierce, "Connecting with the New Global Youth Culture," Lausanne Movement, August 31, 2023, https://lausanne.org/content/lga/2019-03/connecting-with-the-new-global-youth-culture.

their connection to older generations in their own families, communities, and churches.

GENERATIONS DEFINED

To best understand the importance of current trends, it is necessary to consider the source of generational differences. While there are many factors that can contribute to generational cohorts sharing similar perspectives and behaviors, Taylor and Keeter discussed how often age group differences result from three overlapping processes.[54]

The first process in generational identity is life cycle effects. These are the ways that young people may be different from older people today, but they may become more like them when they themselves age. Youth typically demonstrate optimism for the future, adaptability, and desire to improve upon what has been done in the past. As we age, life circumstances tend to result in older individuals being more cautious, realistic, and resistant to change.

Taylor and Keeter explained that period effects are the second indicator in generational differences.[55] Period effects are major events—such as wars, social movements, economic trends, and technological developments—that impact all age groups simultaneously. However, the degree of impact may differ according to their age at the time of the event. Period effects are profound today. Young people are experiencing not only the events that directly affect their local communities, but vicariously, through technology, they are also experiencing wars, tragedies, and trends that are impacting their peers globally. In addition, due to globalization, young people across different demographic groups often experience the same event, such as the COVID-19 pandemic, though the impact may be different based on location.

---

54 Taylor, Paul, and Scott Keeter, eds. 2010. Review of *Millennials: Confident. Connected. Open to Change.* Pew Research Center. https://www.pewresearch.org/wp-content/uploads/sites/3/2010/10/millennials-confident-connected-open-to-change.pdf.
55 Taylor, Paul, and Scott Keeter.

Cohort effects are a third process that results in affinity within generational cohorts.[56] This process involves the trends that can leave a deep impression on youth and young adults as they are developing their core values. The resulting perspectives often stay with them as they move through their life cycle. Values such as secularism, tolerance and individualism are some of the most significant cohort effects for young Millennials (b. 1980-1995), Generation Z (b. 1996-2010), and Generation Alpha (b. after 2010). The idea that there is no absolute truth and therefore no universal morality is prevalent in youth culture today.[57] This is a significant shift from how many older generations across different cultures view the world.

Twenge indicated that today we are experiencing "social generations: those born around the same time who experienced roughly the same culture growing up."[58] This phenomenon is significant when you consider the rate of change in culture today. Cultural change is not new. Peter Drucker explained:

> *Every few hundred years in Western history, there occurs a sharp transformation. Within a few short decades, society--its worldview, its basic values, its social and political structures, its arts, its key institutions--rearranges itself. Fifty years later there is a new world. And the people born then cannot even imagine the world in which their own parents were born. We are currently living through such a transformation.*[59]

The reality today is that cultural transformations that may have remained somewhat confined to local or national cultures, are now resulting in global impact. Cultural change leads to generational differences as each generation effectively grows up in a different culture."[60] In the 21st century, young people globally are growing up

---

56 Taylor, Paul, and Scott Keeter.
57 "What Is the Global Youth Culture."
58 Twenge, *Generations*, 2.
59 Peter Drucker, *Post-Capitalist Society* (New York: Harper Collins, 1993), 1.
60 Twenge, *Generations*, 4.

in a rapidly evolving, interconnected culture very different from that experienced by their parents and grandparents.

IMPLICATIONS FOR THE CHURCH

The profound cultural shift and resulting generational differences globally today have significant implications for the Church. Stieger International indicates that the church struggles to engage younger generations because of the "large cultural gap that exists between the Church and the Global Youth Culture."[61] The Varkey Foundation's Global Citizenship Survey looked at the attitudes, behaviors, and experiences of Generation Z across 20 countries in the first international comparative study of such scale. The Survey found that "religious faith is an important part of less than half of young people's lives globally. Two-fifths (39%) claim religion is of no significance to them at all." This statistic stands in stark contrast to the finding that "84% of young people globally say that technical advancements make them hopeful for the future."[62] The survey further discovered that many young people surveyed have congruent views, highlighting the emerging similarities among Generation Z globally.

One Hope's Global Youth Culture study compiled survey responses from 8,394 teens in 20 countries.[63] The report affirmed global values and trends among young people and offered additional insights for the Church as we seek to engage younger generations. Of the teens surveyed in this study, over half (52%) believe all religions teach equally valid truths.[64] Surprisingly, Christians are just as likely as non-believers to say this. While 43% of teens surveyed self-identified as Christians, only 7% display the beliefs and habits of a

---

[61] "What Is the Global Youth Culture."
[62] Gen Z: Global Citizenship Survey, 2017, Varkey Foundation, accessed January 29, 2021,

https://www.varkeyfoundation.org/what-we-do/research/generation-z-global-citizenship-survey/
[63] Global Youth Culture Report. One Hope. 2020. https://www.globalyouthculture.net/reports/
[64] Global Youth Culture Report, 4.

Committed Christian. The report defines a committed Christian as one who prays and reads the Bible on their own at least weekly and believes the following: God exists and one can have a personal relationship with Him, Jesus is the Son of God, forgiveness of sins is only possible through faith in Jesus Christ, and the Bible is the Word of God.[65]

One Hope's study echoes the findings of Barna's study of young adults in America. "There is a countercultural 10 percent of young Christians whose faith is vibrant and robust...this percentage amounts to just under four million, eighteen - to – twenty nine years-old young adults in the US who follow Jesus and are resiliently faithful."[66] Kinnaman and Matlock described resilient disciples as those who 1) attend church at least monthly and engage with their church more than just attending worship services; 2) trust firmly in the authority of the Bible; 3) are committed to Jesus personally and affirm he was crucified and raised from the dead to conquer sin and death; and 4) express desire to transform the broader society as an outcome of their faith.[67]

The implications of these and other studies on the next generation today present opportunities for the Church. We must be willing to contextualize our ministry approach to the global youth culture. In some contexts, this may mean traditional approaches to ministry need to give way to new, cross-cultural approaches that can effectively engage a new generation with the truth of the gospel.

A second implication is that the young people who are showing up in our churches and ministries represent a precious remnant. While they may bring behaviors or perspectives that are challenging to those who have been in ministry for years, they are seeking God, despite a global youth culture that is antagonistic towards God's truth. Many of them are experiencing isolation, rejection, or opposition as a result of their choice to be a committed Christian and resiliently faithful. Despite the challenges that may exist as the Church engages

---

[65] Global Youth Culture Report, 6.
[66] David Kinnaman and Mark Matlock. Faith for Exiles : 5 Ways for a New Generation to Follow Jesus in Digital Babylon. (Grand Rapids, Mi: Baker Books, 2019), 32.
[67] David Kinnaman and Mark Matlock. *Faith for Exiles : 5 Ways for a New Generation to Follow Jesus in Digital Babylon.* (Grand Rapids, Mi: Baker Books, 2019), 33.

younger generations who have grown up in a different culture than the previous generations, it is an honor to steward and shepherd the young people God is raising up for such a time as this.

NEXT GEN CONTRIBUTIONS

As young Millennials, Generation Z, and Generation Alpha engage in God's global work, they bring unique skills and perspectives. For example, their understanding of generational values and views in one cultural context may equip them to more effectively engage peers in other contexts. While many trends in the global youth culture may not align with biblical truth, for those young people committed to following Christ, we see God redeeming and using generational traits in unique and powerful ways for His Kingdom purposes in the 21st century.

In a recent study, young people between the ages of 18-30 who are considering or currently pursuing global missions were asked, "In what ways do you believe God has uniquely equipped your generation to contribute to His mission globally?"[68] The following overview are examples of their responses. They reflect some of the ways God is preparing and using the next generation.

COMMITMENT (THAT HAS ENDURED TESTING!)

David Kinnaman and Mark Matlock, in their book *Faith for Exiles*, contended that "today's society is especially and insidiously faith repellent."[69] They reported that it is hard to grow resilient faith in this generation of young people growing up in a post-Christian culture.[70] Gen Z and Millennial believers who have been raised in post-Christian contexts often sense this. The following comments

---

[68] Next Generation in Mission Aviation Report, IAMA and Leading Tomorrow, 2024.
[69] David Kinnaman and Mark Matlock. *Faith for Exiles*, 15.
[70] David Kinnaman and Mark Matlock. *Faith for Exiles*, 15.

from young adults reflect how they see their commitment being both tested and resilient as they seek to follow Christ today:

> *Young people growing up in the States are having their faith challenged more than former generations. I hope this daily defense of faith can prepare us more for life on the mission field.*
>
> *When we fully buy into a mission, we are sold. Once we are able to detach from the distractions of culture...we are able to fully focus on Christ, be strongly grounded, and put in the work.*[71]
>
> *In a culture where everyone is trying to tell us what the truth is, we really have to be convinced. But, when we are convinced that something is true and real, we cling to it and we will fight to defend it.*

TECHNOLOGY SKILLS

The oldest members of Generation Z were early adolescents when the iPhone was introduced in 2007 and high school students when the iPad entered the scene in 2010.[72] In addition to being the first generation to grow up with interactive technologies in their back pockets, Gen Z, with birth years beginning in 1996, was the first generation to grow up after the Internet was commercialized in 1995. As a result, younger generations today tend to be tech savvy and appreciate the potential of technology as seen in the following comments:

---

71 Next Generation in Mission Aviation Report, IAMA and Leading Tomorrow, 2024.
72 Jean Twenge. *IGen : Why Today's Super-Connected Kids Are Growing up Less Rebellious, More Tolerant, Less Happy--and Completely Unprepared for Adulthood (and What This Means for the Rest of Us).* (New York, Ny: Atria Paperback, 2018), p. 24.

From Womb to Tomb

Technology has really connected the world, and the younger generations have embraced that more wholeheartedly than the older. That is a tool that could spread the gospel like wildfire!

I think missions has changed a lot in the last 30 years, and with technology there are a lot more opportunities for new ways of serving and reaching people for the sake of the Gospel.[73]

GLOBALLY CONNECTED AND AWARE

As discussed at the beginning of this chapter, young people are growing up in a global youth culture. As a result, they tend to be globally connected and aware at a young age of what is happening around the world. This has several implications as the next generation engages in ministry, as discussed in the following insights from young people in missions:

We have become even more interconnected on a global level and this ability to know what is going on around the world helps us see more directly how we can contribute by using the gifts, skills, and passions we have. Also, there is more of a shift occurring with mission work in developing countries looking at not only how needs can be met and the Gospel spread, but how can this be done in a sustainable way and carried forward by national staff as well. This is SO important!

We have grown up used to a more connected world. I think it's in our nature to stay connected wherever we are. This could help bring more awareness to the church of the needs of missionaries and ministries on the field reaching the lost.[74]

---

[73] Next Generation in Mission Aviation Report, IAMA and Leading Tomorrow, 2024.
[74] Next Generation in Mission Aviation Report, IAMA and Leading Tomorrow, 2024.

STRONG EMPATHY

Twenge noted, "Individualism is behind the most fundamental changes of the last few decades."[75] She explained, "Technology makes individualism possible."[76] Well into the 20th century, so much time was spent globally on simply existing. As a result, little time was left to focus on feelings and individual experiences. In many cultures today, electricity, grocery stores, access to water, and technology have reduced the time spent on the drudgery of life and given people more time to think about one's own emotions and experiences, as well as those of others. This increased focus on individuals, along with the global awareness mentioned above, has contributed to a high value on inclusion and empathy in younger generations. When leveraged in biblical ways, this strong empathy can contribute to the next generation's ability to connect and serve globally, as evidenced in the comments below:

> *We're an "include everyone" generation, which contributes to the desire to take the gospel to every nation.*
>
> *God has given my generation a gift for empathy and sympathy. We are often more aware of our emotions and the emotions of others than previous generations.*
>
> *I think my generation is generally good at "seeing" people, rather than focusing on tasks to get done.*
>
> *We are more empathetic and I believe that makes us...adept at learning and understanding new cultures.*[77]

This strong empathy and desire for inclusion effectively positions the next generation for polycentric mission and leadership. Braithwaite and Handley describe polycentric leadership as "leadership that

---

75 Twenge. *IGen*, p. 94.
76 Twenge, *Generations*, 11.
77 Next Generation in Mission Aviation Report, IAMA and Leading Tomorrow, 2024.

functions across multiple spheres of influence, including geography, ethnicity, age, region, gender, and nationality. Polycentric leadership has many centres of authority or importance. In other words, it is a diversified leadership, from everyone to everywhere."[78] The next generation is uniquely equipped and positioned to live and lead a polycentric approach to missions.

FOR SUCH A TIME AS THIS

As younger generations today prepare and participate in God's global work alongside believers from around the world, new complexities and opportunities must be considered. Rapid and on-going change will likely require diverse and adaptable approaches to leadership and ministry. Doug Harrison, Director of Strategy at MAF explained, "As raw material, we acknowledge that the emerging generation needs engagement and mentoring. But not to fashion them into a replicant of my generation, but a generation prepared for what is emerging over the horizon of history."[79] This is our challenge as we prepare the next generation for their season of ministry and leadership.

In today's context, it is important to consider how we may be relying on our strategies or on tried-and-true methods that have consistently worked over time. We may have developed organizational cultures and processes that feel familiar and comfortable.[80] However, in the midst of the cultural shifts that are occurring today, we need fresh insight and guidance from the Holy Spirit on how to move into the future. In their book, Spiritual Leadership, Henry and Richard Blackaby stated, "The challenge for today's leaders is to discern the difference between the latest leadership fads and timeless truths es-

---

[78] Michaela Brathwaite and Joseph W. Handley. "What Is Polycentric Mission Leadership?" Lausanne Movement, Sep. 20, 2022. https://lausanne.org/about/blog/what-is-polycentric-mission-leadership

[79] Harrison, Doug. Email Correspondence. August 26, 2021.

[80] Jolene Erlacher and Katy White, Mobilizing Gen Z: Challenges and Opportunities for the Global Age of Missions (William Carey Publishing, 2022), p. 154.

tablished by God."[81] While we do need to consider valuable research, generational trends, and leadership tools, ultimately there is no substitute for getting on our knees and seeking the Lord's wisdom for this time.

In my work on generational research, I have sometimes questioned my ability to engage our current context effectively. I can identify with Esther who was unsure of her ability to respond to the challenges of her day. Mordecai's words to her are relevant for us today. "Who knows but that we have come into our current positions and relationships for such a time as this?[82] I am continually reminded that God has chosen each of us for the season of ministry into which He has called us. There is great encouragement in trusting His guidance, equipping, and faithfulness as we engage His Kingdom purposes across generations!

---

81 Blackaby, Henry T, and Richard Blackaby. 2001. Spiritual Leadership: Moving People on to God's Agenda. South Africa: Struik Christian Books. p. 14.

82 Esther 4:14 NIV

Bridging the Gap: Embracing Intergenerational Leadership in Christian Ministry

Micaela Braithwaite

'We know that there are over 60 million Gen Z workers, and they are well on their way to becoming the most influential group in the workplace.' Generation Z are viewed not just as the future of the workforce and economy, but as an important role in the workplace today. Yet how few Christian leadership teams are intentional in cultivating intergenerational teams and including younger generations in the decision-making process.

According to the Harvard Business Review, 'Aging leadership structures need to involve less experienced talent in order to rebalance the tensions of experience versus curiosity and of efficient execution versus bold exploration. Striving towards intergenerational leadership can accelerate companies' efforts to build a sustainable future—and unlock competitive advantages at the same time.'

The marketplace has seen the importance of intergenerational leadership in recent years and studies show that companies that focus on intergenerational leadership perform better.[83] For the first time we have five generations in the workplace simultaneously. That creates both opportunity and challenge in the workplace, and they are seeking to capitalize on it. Yet the beauty of intergenerational leadership is not a new concept nor is it a secular idea. The Bible has many accounts of the importance of multi-generational leadership. Moses and Paul will be briefly highlighted as two examples.

LESSONS FROM MOSES

As far back as the time of Moses, we can learn that different generations have different gifts and perspectives to offer that complement one another.

Exodus chapter 18 illustrates how through heeding the wisdom and advice of an older person Moses was able to be more effective in his calling. We often think of Moses as a young man at this point in his leadership, but he was well beyond 80 years (Exodus 7:7), and still benefited from having an older experienced leader speak into his life. Not only did he have someone who gave input into his leadership, but Moses led together with his two siblings as well as the seventy leaders he appointed as a result of his father-in-law's advice. He also mentored Joshua as his personal aide and successor, inviting him into important missions like scouting out the Promised Land (Numbers 13) and ultimately leading the Israelites into it.

Moses included Joshua in the source of his leadership success—time spent in the presence of God (Exodus 33:11). He invited Joshua to participate in every aspect of the ministry alongside him and gave

---

[83] Hennelly, Debra and Schurman, Bradley. "Bridging Generational Divides in Your Workplace." Harvard Business Review, January 2023, https://hbr.org/2023/01/bridging-generational-divides-in-your-workplace

him authority as a leader, ensuring that he and Joshua led together on multiple occasions.[84]

Through listening to the advice of his father-in-law and raising a team of people around him, Moses was able to share the burden of leadership while also inviting others into the opportunity to serve and develop their gifts. In this way not only did he have greater leadership capacity, but the whole community benefited from the shared leadership and even when Moses was unable to see the vision come to fruition, he had raised up leaders who were strong and capable for the task. Ultimately, the time came for Moses to step aside and entrust the mission to the next generation of capable leaders (Joshua 1).

THE EXAMPLE OF PAUL TO TIMOTHY

Likewise, Paul invited Timothy and included him in his ministry even as a young adult. By studying the relationship between Paul and Timothy and his family heritage, Oladotun Anthony Akinsulire highlights the significance of the community of faith in transmitting a sustainable faith to the next generation.[85]

Timothy had a rich heritage of faith from his grandmother Lois and mother Eunice (2 Timothy 1:5). Even at a very young age Timothy had a glowing reputation of piety and virtue among the community of believers in Iconium and Lystra. He had been religiously educated and was carefully trained in the knowledge of the Scriptures, and was therefore positioned and well prepared for the work to which God now called him. Timothy was to become not just one of Paul's most reliable compatriots but one of his closest friends (1 Corinthians 4:17).

---

84 Butler, Trent C. Joshua. *Word Biblical Commentary 7*. Waco, TX: Thomas Nelson, 1983. Accessed March 2023.https://www.proquest.com/openview/ffc6ab01a184d829 7f5b6f5e29609e1e/1?pq-origsite=gscholar&cbl=18750&diss=y

85 Akinsulire, Oladotun. "An Intergenerational Approach to a Sustainable Youth Ministry (Acts 16:1-3) in an African Context." *Sapientia Foundation Journal of Education, Sciences and Gender Studies (SFJESGS)*, vol. 3, no. 1, 2021, pp. 372–375. ISSN: 2734-2514 (Online).

Paul recognized the need of raising up and commissioning young leaders and demonstrated it in entrusting Timothy for the missionary task to the Aegean shores. Paul was deliberate and strategic in creating opportunities to integrate a young leader like Timothy into the life and mission of the church. Young as he was, Paul's vision for Timothy was not just as a consumer of the faith, nor was he assigned to menial tasks, but Paul encouraged him to not allow others look down on his age (1 Timothy 4:12), but to stand firm in his faith and calling (1 Timothy 6:12).

Oladotun concludes that regardless of age, intergenerational ministry serves to enable the whole church to benefit from each individual's God-given gifts and enables Christians to fully live out being the body of Christ and the family of faith.[86]

GENERATIONS AND THEIR UNIQUE CONTRIBUTIONS

The workplace today is more diverse than ever before with five generations working side-by-side. We may tend to think of generations in terms of succession where each generation represents the next rung of the ladder, however we should think of it more like the strands of a rope, where together each strand makes a stronger cord.

Each generation is defined by a set of characteristics and experiences that shape their worldview, values, and behaviors. Some key characteristics commonly associated with each generation are briefly outlined below.

TRADITIONALISTS

Traditionalists (born before 1946) generally value hard work, duty, loyalty, and respect for authority. They grew up during the Great Depression and World War II, leading to a strong sense of patriotism

---

[86] Ibid.

and sacrifice. They have resilience and perspectives unique to their experience. This generation prefers formal, face-to-face or written communication.

BABY BOOMERS

Baby Boomers (born 1946-1964) value optimism, personal fulfilment, and work-life balance. They are the generation born during the population surge in the years immediately following World War II. They witnessed significant social and cultural changes, including the civil rights movement and the rise of feminism. They prefer communicating through phone calls and meetings, and value personal connections.

GENERATION X

Generation X (born 1965-1980) values independence, work-life balance, and entrepreneurship. They have lived through economic uncertainty and rapid technological advancements, such as the rise of the internet. They are known as a resourceful and independent generation. They are generally comfortable with technology however they have had to adapt to rapidly advancing technological developments and are most comfortable with email communication and text messaging.

MILLENNIALS

Millennials (born 1981-1996) value diversity, social justice, work flexibility, and technology. They grew up in the digital age, faced economic challenges such as student debt and the Great Recession. They are currently established as a pivotal force in the global marketplace. Regarding communication, Millennials prefer digital communication channels, valuing authenticity and transparency.

GENERATION Z

Generation Z (born 1997-2012) value diversity, social activism, individuality, and technology. This cohort was born into a digital world, exposed to social media and global connectivity from a young age and are instinctive when it comes to technology and media. Their communication style is highly digital-native, and they prefer messaging apps and social media for communication.

GENERATION ALPHA

Generation Alpha (born after 2012) value self-expression and individuality. They are 'digital natives', surrounded by technology from birth. Generation Alpha is expected to be the most technologically adept generation yet, with even greater fluency in digital devices and platforms compared to previous generations. As they are still very young, the full characteristics and traits of Generation Alpha are still emerging and evolving.

Any large generational gaps in leadership teams results in missing out on the important and unique contributions that each generation has to offer and what God has entrusted to that generation, as well as reducing any oversight or blind spots of a particular group. Understanding these generational characteristics can help teams tailor their strategies, communication, and engagement approaches to effectively reach and connect with different age groups and a wider audience.

WHAT IS MEANT BY THE TERM 'INTERGENERATIONAL'?

James White uses the term intergenerational to describe 'two or more age groups of people in a religious community together learning/growing/living in faith through in-common experiences, parallel learning, contributive occasions and interactive sharing'.[87] Allan Harkness says that 'intentional intergenerational strategies are those in which an integral part of the process of faith communities encourages interpersonal interactions across generational boundaries, and in which a sense of mutuality and equality is encouraged between participants.'[88]

Bambang Budijanto draws a distinction between the terms multi-generational and intergenerational leadership.[89] Many organizations, churches and teams are multi-generational, meaning that there may be youth, young adults, middle-aged, and seniors, however intergenerational is unique in that it requires intentional engagement between the generations. Intergenerational leadership involves different generations in the leadership team making decisions together. This is not just assigning tasks to each member of the team, rather together they engage one another in the decision-making process. This both shapes and grows the leadership team, and also allows for more dynamic and broadly informed decision-making.

Fostering this kind of leadership team requires an added level of humility across the leadership. Many times leadership teams may think they are intergenerational by inviting a younger member into the team, only in order to resort to job-assignment, or to have the younger member act as an observer. To genuinely foster intergenerational leadership, teams must strive for an inclusive environment where each member has the opportunity to contribute according to their gifting and function.

---

[87] Allen, Holly and Ross, Christine. (2012). *Intergenerational Christian Formation*. Downers Grove: InterVarsity Press.
[88] Ibid.
[89] Budijanto, Bambang. (2021, February 28). *Intergenerational Leadership* [Webinar]. Asia Evangelical Alliance. https://www.youtube.com/watch?v=t9UM2FmqhNs

LEADERSHIP IS A GIFT TO BE NURTURED

Appointments to leadership should be derived from gifts and not primarily from seniority or even experience. Budijanto believes that the key to effective intergenerational leadership is leadership not by age but by function.[90]

What a fresh perspective this is to the traditional approach in many global contexts where younger, less-experienced leaders are sidelined by older leaders, resulting in a power-struggle. On the other hand, consider many modern contexts where older, wise leaders are disregarded as no longer relevant and their wealth of experience, research, and insight is not utilized. Both instances result in complacency instead of a wonderful harmony of older generations and younger generations complementing one another's strengths and making up for where the other is lacking. This is the beauty of intergenerational leadership in mission.

Perhaps part of the reason for poor leadership is lack of intergenerational nurturing of younger leaders. Without the depth of more senior leaders to complement their inexperience, younger leaders are often left to the decision making process without first being grafted into a team and allowing them to learn, make mistakes, and even fail.

Spiritual formation is a lifelong process. Jamie Coats argues that for healthy spiritual formation to occur, the older generations need the passion, exuberance, and new insights of the younger generations, while the younger generations need the wisdom, experience, and expertise of the older generations. All generations need regular interaction and involvement with the other generations in community in order to mature in a spiritually-healthy manner, and in order to develop a healthy self-identity.[91]

Likewise, when intergenerational integration fails to happen in leadership, we find stagnant and undeveloped gifts of leadership in

---

90 Ibid.
91 Coates, Jamie R., "Join the Band: Benefits of Engaging Intergenerational Volunteers in the Local Church Worship Ministry" (2019). Doctoral Dissertations and Projects. 2070. https://digitalcommons.liberty.edu/doctoral/2070

young leaders. Talking about the effects of age-segregation in the local church context, Coats makes an argument for the limiting effect it has on the generation in question to the role of consumer. 'The Christian faith is in danger of being understood by youth as a commodity to consume like a good cup of coffee, not a community in which to belong and participate.' Likewise, if leadership is only affirmed in those who have executive levels of experience it leaves younger leaders as the critical consumer.[92]

CHALLENGES TO INTERGENERATIONAL LEADERSHIP

THE GENERATION GAP— COMMUNICATION

The generational gap often shows itself most clearly in the form of communication, or rather mis-communication. Diverse teams of leaders need to be aware of what is being communicated—as well as what isn't and how that affects the different generations involved. In recent years there has been a focus on personality tests and psychometric tests to boost team function. Likewise, studying how different generations communicate and being aware of how communication breaks down is important in building an inter-generational leadership team. In *Learning to Maximize Your Leadership Potential*, Michael Gourgues states that how and why a leader communicates can be just as important as what is communicated.[93] 'Strategic communication

---

92 Ibid.
93 Momeny, Leonard & Gourgues, Michael. (2019). Learning to Maximize your Leadership Communication. 7, 33-35.

implies that leaders must ensure that they are communicating the right message to the right people at the right time.[94]'

Varying levels of comfort and proficiency with technology can create barriers to communication and information sharing among different age groups, along with generational stereotypes, where preconceived notions or stereotypes about certain generations can hinder collaboration and trust among team members.

THE AUTHORITY GAP—POWER

In leadership there is often an authority gap between younger and older leaders. Shared leadership means shared power and authority. It also means shared responsibility which can be difficult for leaders to hand over especially if they don't feel confident in the abilities of other leaders or they feel ownership of the vision.

Many societies are still highly patriarchal. Patriarchy is a form of male domination based on the powerful role of the father as head of the household and can be expressed in a multitude of ways. The forms of control and subordination characteristic of patriarchal practices cut across cultural and religious boundaries.[95] Often patriarchal societies are also societies where respect is paramount, especially in positions of leadership. This may mean that any changes to the leadership structure are viewed as a threat and any younger leaders are seen to be agents of change in an established team. Traditional hierarchical leadership structures may not resonate with younger generations who prefer more collaborative and inclusive leadership approaches.

Other challenges may include differing values and priorities. Each generation may prioritize different values and goals, leading to potential conflicts or disagreements over organizational direction or

---

94 Ibid.
95 Akinsulire, Oladotun. "An Intergenerational Approach to a Sustainable Youth Ministry (Acts 16:1-3) in an African Context." *Sapientia Foundation Journal of Education, Sciences and Gender Studies (SFJESGS)*, vol. 3, no. 1, 2021, pp. 372–375. ISSN: 2734-2514 (Online).

decision-making. Furthermore, elder generations may be resistant to change or new ideas, while younger generations may feel frustrated by perceived stagnation or resistance to innovation.

OVERCOMING INTER-GENERATIONAL CHALLENGES

While the challenges of building effective intergenerational leadership teams may come naturally, Christ-following leaders ought to foster the following postures in order to reduce the amount of friction caused between team members.

HUMILITY

Leadership teams need to cultivate a culture of trust and accountability. Leadership teams must cultivate a culture of humility, where individuals are open to learning from one another and value diverse perspectives. This includes acknowledging the unique contributions of each generation and recognizing that no one has all the answers.

LISTENING

Effective communication is essential for bridging generational gaps. Leaders should actively listen to the ideas, concerns, and feedback of team members from all age groups, creating an environment where everyone feels heard and valued. Encouraging a culture of transparency and inclusivity can help bridge generational gaps and build trust within the team.

PATIENCE

Recognize that making mistakes is a natural part of the learning process, especially when navigating intergenerational dynamics. Leaders should demonstrate patience and understanding, providing support and guidance as team members adapt to new ways of working together.

CURIOSITY AND THE WILLINGNESS TO LEARN

Foster a culture of curiosity and continuous learning within the team. Encourage team members to embrace a "learner leader" mindset, where they actively seek out opportunities to expand their knowledge and understanding of different perspectives.

MUTUALITY AND FRIENDSHIP

Intergenerational relationships go beyond mentorship and aims for genuine friendship. Mentorship is often one-sided where the mentor is expected to impart knowledge, and the mentee to receive. The structure of inter-generational leadership emphasizes missional friendships, which are side-by-side, facing outwards by engaging common interests towards a common goal.

This kind of friendship is mutually beneficial. When both parties intentionally foster trust, humility, respect, empathy, and reconciliation, the relational bridge can become strong enough to sustain difficult conversations instead of fostering superficial empowerment. This can lead to authentic intergenerational partnerships for global mission, because the mission benefits from what each has to offer.[96]

By embracing these principles of humility, listening, patience, curiosity, and mutuality, leadership teams can effectively navigate inter-generational challenges and create a more inclusive and collaborative work environment.

---

96 Braithwaite, M. "God's Purpose in Intergenerational Leadership" Lausanne Movement, [5 July 2023], https://lausanne.org/about/blog/gods-purpose-in-intergenerational-leadership

BUILDING A BETTER TEAM

Intergenerational leadership in Christian ministry and mission is not merely about building a sustainable succession plan, it is about enriching the decision-making process and developing and shaping each leader to be more broadly equipped to make decisions that engage different perspectives. Inter-generational mission leadership communicates that leadership has no boundary of life stage but is rather part of lifelong spiritual formation.

The biblical examples of Moses and Paul highlight the importance of intergenerational leadership in fulfilling God's mission. From Moses' mentorship of Joshua to Paul's investment in Timothy, these leaders understood the value of nurturing the next generation of leaders and creating opportunities for them to thrive. By following their example and embracing the principles of humility, active listening, patience, curiosity, and mutuality, Christian leadership teams can overcome intergenerational challenges and create a more vibrant and effective ministry that reflects the diversity and richness of God's kingdom.

Intergenerational leadership is not easy, and it will take a little more intention to overcome some of the challenges, but it invites all to engage their gifts and serve the global body of Christ for the sake of God's mission on earth.

III.
Case Studies

Out of the Mouths of Babes: God Speaking in the Lives of Children

Editor's Note: The following two testimonies were written by Bishop and Sophie. They are brother and sister, children of Tony and Zen Tira. Their contribution to the book is offered as example of how God is at work in the lives of the children and young people among us.

ACCEPTING GOD AS A KID

I've been playing and learning hockey for eight years in different positions from goalie to left wing to a defenseman. For the past three years, I've been playing for KC (Knights of Columbus), after starting with the Lil Oilers and Timbits when I was 5. I was number 13 this year, and I played in four different tournaments in my seven-month-long season, winning bronze in my latest tournament against four other teams. I disciple those on my teams, wanting my friends to come to know God the way I do. And I dream of being in the NHL when I'm older and taking my dad to all of my games because I started because of him. He used to play all kinds of different sports except for hockey, but it is also his favorite sport to watch, and he has passed his dreams down to me.

I'm in the sixth grade and I've been playing ukulele at school for the past three years at my school, even having the opportunity to play at the jubilee auditorium this year with my other classmates filling the auditorium all the way. I took up this instrument first because my sister plays and because I wanted to learn something new.

My family introduced me to Jesus since I was born. I've been going to church my whole life, and my dad became a pastor like his father before him. I've accepted Jesus from such a young age I can't even remember. I began to help out with my family's church—called Supper Club—almost four years ago, when we started online because of COVID in 2020. Last summer, we met up and I received God and his Spirit, getting baptized in a pool at my tita's [aunt's] house.

I've been influenced by my family ever since I could remember. The first job I ever wanted was influenced by my father, wanting to be a pastor/chef, being in awe of him and all the things I've been able to watch him do. My grandparents also have helped me experience God as I've grown up, from my grandma doing Bible study with me and my sister to just taking care of us and learning that you can pray for any and everything. I've experienced my grandparents' love in many different ways, especially in their hospitality, cooking, and their driving us to all the places we need to be. My family makes an effort for me to love God as they do, from all the Bibles they've given me to watching them discipline those around them even when it's hard. They are generous and they pray for me even when they are the ones that need the prayer. In noticing that, I've been able to see all the ways that God works in us and all of our family throughout the generations.

TESTIMONY OF A PK

I'm 15 years old and in grade 9. I've been a PK, aka pastor's kid, since I was around 5 or 6, helping my parents and their ministries since then.

Ever since I became a PK, I've known exactly who are the people who influenced me. I'm continuously learning from my amazing parents, who have been teaching me ever since I can remember, not only the Bible, but manners and their importance, making me grateful for who I am and how I was raised every day. And in being a PK of a PK, I have also been taught things by my grandparents, things that I don't think I would have learned if I had grown up any differently. My grandma is constantly praying and teaching people, showing how much she cares and loves to take care of those around her. And my grandpa wants to share about everything, trying to pass on his wisdom, and my other grandparents show their love in cooking and gifts and taking care of us ever since I can remember.

I am a very creative and different person to most people you would meet my age, but I take pride in the things I love. I love anything to do with music, as it is something that makes me happy when everything I'm feeling is the opposite. And as much as I love listening to music, I also love to play it. I'm a self-taught musician in guitar and ukulele, as well as being a singer. I go to music class with some of my friends from school for fun, where I get to grow in the instruments I play even more. I perform two or three times during the school year. I also play on the worship team at my church once a month. In my free time, if I'm not watching something on Netflix or just on TV, I'm doing something crafty, like making bracelets or crocheting shirts or even writing. I love working on things. I also love to read and to cook. One of the best memories with my grandma is learning to cook eggs with her, and I also love cooking with my other grandma and my dad. It is a very important thing to me and my family, growing up with that quality time.

I don't know exactly who I want to be as I grow up, but I do know the things I love that are going to help me find out, like caring and helping people. One of the best feelings is watching others healing, even when you're not, and the creativity in the things I love to do. As I grow, my grandma asks me what I dream of, and–just like her–I dream of being a friend of God. I don't know what I want to do, but my family definitely has taken a great part of it and are influencing it.

I received God as my Lord and Savior when I was 9 years old, in the middle of the night with my dad and mom. I got baptized a few weeks later, right before I turned 10. I received God and got baptized the second I learned what it meant to be loved by him. Even though I was 9, I got to learn of the great things that he has in store for me, and the endless love he has for me and my family, and, no matter what, I will be ok as long as I am with him.

In growing up with constant love and affection in so many different ways, and taking up all the things I do, I truly couldn't do it without the people around me, whether it be my family or friends or just people I pass by on the street. I've really learned more than I could have ever known I would. If you'd asked where I thought I'd be right now even a week ago, I've been pushing through, learning through it all, like I've been taught my whole life.

Being a Tsinoy Gen Z: Struggling With Language, Hybridity, And Identity

Johann Sven Lee Uytanlet

ABSTRACT:

This chapter is a story of the author's personal journey of being a Chinese Filipino who is from Generation Z. This chapter will explore the unique challenges and experiences that come with it.

INTRODUCTION

I am remarkably resentful about the timing of the pandemic. I was in grade 11, and our class had to do some plays as part of our requirements. There were three groups and three plays in total in the class. Although I have forgotten most of the details of each story, I still remember that the whole class agreed to change the script to create a "cinematic universe" where all of the stories and scripts given by our teacher were somehow interconnected. I was the director of one of the plays, so I had the privilege to try and edit the script to make it appear that all the plays were a part of one big story. Although the writing was amateur, the experience was delightful. I highly appreciate all the actors for their phenomenal acting and for making the play come to life.

When the second play ended, we were very excited for the last play to cap off the story of our class's "cinematic universe." We would be able to see the culmination of our work. The play was supposed to premier the next day. However, I woke up with the news that there would be no classes for the next two weeks because of the Covid-19 pandemic lockdown. After that, there was news that classes would become virtual indefinitely. Everything started to shift online, from academics to socialization. Although these structures and applications like social media, online platforms for classes, and online shopping already existed, they were not as ubiquitous. My fellow Gen Z's and I have been quite affected by this takeover of the internet and the digital age. There are good and bad aspects to this digitalization. Nevertheless, this takeover was inevitable because it would have happened eventually. The pandemic merely accelerated this change.

I want to share my story of being a Gen Z and a Chinese Filipino. A Gen Z is born between 1995-2012. I was born in 2003 to Samson and Juliet Uytanlet. That makes me a Gen Z. I am a Chinese Filipino born in the Philippines. I am Chinese by ethnicity and Filipino by citizenship. There is another term that is popularly used to describe Chinese Filipinos, which is "Tsinoy." Tsinoy means Tsinong (Chinese) Pinoy (Filipino). This chapter will highlight my struggles as a Tsinoy Gen Z in learning languages, adjusting to different environments, and finding my identity.

1. LIFE IN AMERICA AS A TSINOY AND AS A GEN Z

When I was four years old, my parents pursued their education in the United States. I moved with them and lived in Wilmore, Kentucky from 2007 to 2013. I spent a significant portion of my childhood in that small city with only a few thousand residents. Life in the United States was simple but great. My mother tongue is Minnanhua (sometimes referred to as "Hokkien"). It is a Chinese dialect originating from Fujian. Moving to America, it was quite an adjustment to learn and be fluent in English. One time, my nursery teacher visited me at home, but mainly to talk with my parents, because I was speaking to her in Minnanhua in school. I thought everyone else knew the language I spoke so I talked to everyone how I talked with my parents at home. Thankfully, by watching English cartoons and with many friends speaking English with me, I was able to learn English fairly quickly.

My parents and I are trilingual. At home, we would communicate using an amalgamation of English, Filipino, and Minnanhua. Sometimes, even within one sentence, we would use words from each of the three languages. Other times we would use the grammatical structures of one language while fully using the words of another language. When I was young, this setup made it quite difficult for me to learn how to speak one language fluently. It took me a while to distinguish which words belonged to which language. There were times I would think an English word was a Filipino word or a Filipino word was a Minnanhua word. This further exacerbated my confusion. Even to this day I still have some issues distinguishing which words are Filipino and which ones are from Minnanhua. I would talk in Minnanhua and use a Filipino word but with a Chinese intonation only to find out later that, it was a Filipino word. Growing up, I mostly dealt with this confusion by choosing to master English. I still understood most of the words from Minnanhua and Filipino when my parents were talking to me. However, while in America I mostly replied in straight English even when my parents talked to me in Minnanhua or Filipino.

A particular advantage to highlight when living in a household that speaks three different languages is having access to a wider vocabulary. Finding words in very specific contexts is easier to a certain extent. For example, in Filipino, the term kilig means something similar to the phrase "feeling butterflies in your stomach." The neat part is that the term is one word, not a phrase, and it is a verb. With this in mind, accurately expressing our ideas to each other is much simpler.

Another important highlight during my stay in America was that I was able to make many friends from different countries. We stayed in the student housing of Asbury Theological Seminary. They had a good number of international students, and many of them were our neighbors. Most of my friends were the children of those students, and we were all from a variety of ethnic backgrounds.

In my neighborhood, no one else was from the Philippines, but we have Chinese neighbors from Taiwan. Even though most of the other kids looked and lived differently, we learned to look past our differences and see our similarities. Although I am not extremely extroverted, this experience has helped me make connections with almost anyone. As I spent time with them, the more we rubbed off onto each other, I developed a habit of bowing from my Korean and Japanese friends. Sometimes they greet each other using a small nod of the head, and I started to follow their lead. Even to this day I still nod my head as a greeting to others. It is almost reflexive at this point.

During my stay in Wilmore, I acquired some parts of American culture, taste, and even their accent. I joined their festivities like the Fourth of July and Thanksgiving. I love American food, like burgers, mashed potatoes, pancakes, cereals, and a lot more. I am especially fond of their serving sizes. I developed a southern accent as I lived in Kentucky. Unfortunately, I lost the accent over time when we moved back to the Philippines.

I studied at Wilmore Elementary School, in Jessamine County, Kentucky. It is a public school with great teachers and facilities. I did not feel discriminated against at all by the school or by my peers.

This experience of living in the United States has made me feel very "hybrid." I felt somewhat out of place. I did not feel alienated because people did not want to associate with me. I felt like an outsider because I felt I did not completely fit in, in a cultural sense rather than in a social sense. There are times when my values, language, and traditions do not completely align with the people around me. Of course, the only person who would think the same way as one's self is themselves. However, I longed for a truer sense of belonging.

From a Christian perspective, believers also have this sort of feeling, like being in limbo. We live in this world but are not fully part of it. We are citizens of heaven, but also have citizenships in the countries where we live. Not to say that being a child of God does not come first, but it would be strange to completely deny the effects of the circumstances of one's birth.

2. LIFE IN THE PHILIPPINES AS A TSINOY AND AS A GEN Z

After my parents finished their studies, we moved back to the Philippines. I had a major culture shock. School felt more hostile and unwelcoming. The teachers came across as more aggressive and stricter compared to my teachers from Wilmore. They spoke straight Filipino in some parts of their lectures, and my Filipino language skills were not as adept as my English language skills at that time. There was a major shift in the environment from a developed country to a developing country. Poverty is much more apparent and seen easily in Metro Manila compared with Jessamine County. A shift from joining a megachurch in America to joining a mid-sized Chinese church in the Philippines. The Chinese churches were bilingual, and they spoke both English and Minnanhua. Some Chinese churches had services where the only language they used in their preachings was Minnanhua. Although my parents spoke with me in Minnanhua and Filipino while we were in Wilmore, I was not fluent in these languages as I was in English and I did not have much time to practice them outside of home. At one point, I could not understand the messages because of the language barrier. I had to slowly relearn Minnanhua from my relatives as my grandmother's primary language was Minnanhua. I had to join a special class in high school to learn the Filipino language. I also had a big adjustment in dealing with my extended family. For context, both of my parents have eleven siblings. A majority of those siblings have children, and some of their children even have children. I had to learn almost seventy names in such a short time. Even to this day, I have some trouble remembering who is who. There were so many adjustments that I needed to go through for me to get used to coming back to live in the Philippines, taking one step at a time in every aspect of my life.

It was not only in America that I felt a sense of being out of place, but also in the Philippines. This feeling of being out of place came from being a Tsinoy. As a Chinese living in the Philippines, I feel as if I am not as Filipino as the locals in a cultural sense. Many of the traditions I practice and beliefs I have are Chinese in origin. This is not to say that I do not also subscribe to Filipino traditions and beliefs, but I do not subscribe to one or the other exclusively and fully. At the same time, I do not feel Chinese like I am part of China. I have met many people from China, and their command of the language and their values and beliefs are way different compared to what me and my fellow Chinese in the Philippines have. Being Tsinoy feels like I can enter, at most, only partially inside both worlds but never be truly in one.

When I came back to the Philippines, I had this wrong notion that I would find a community that would give me a truer sense of belonging, that I was seeking. I had a line of thought where if I meet people who are also Chinese from the Philippines I would relate and feel more at home with them. However, I realized it was not about finding people who are similar to you whether it be in culture, ethnicity, interests, age, and more. It is about finding people who accept you regardless of your cultural heritage or ethnic origin. I have a set of experiences in my life that makes me feel like I am not "part" of a greater community, culturally speaking. However, everyone is unique and different in their own way, and it will be surprising to find someone who has lived a similar life as you. I also realize that this sense of belonging can be found in the community of believers, and the person who unites the community is Jesus. It is this "fictive community" that can truly provide a real community.

The church as a community is essential to my spiritual formation. However, my parents are the primary influencers of my spirituality. From a very young age, I have been always praying to God. This is thanks to my parents teaching me to pray and rely on God. Without them, I would not have decided to be baptized at the age of 9. I remember my parents and Sunday School teachers asking me if I was sure that I would want to be baptized. I said I was because I wanted to follow Jesus. In my high school years, I joined a devotional group where I had opportunities to lead devotions. This group also helped in my spiritual growth as I learned to study the Word of God. During the pandemic, I joined an online youth Bible study group where I continued to grow in my faith.

3. THE IMPACT OF THE INTERNET

With access to the internet, my experience of meeting people from different backgrounds may be more universal than it might seem to Gen Z. When the pandemic hit, I joined an online Pokémon community in Discord as I craved for social interaction. I digitally encountered many people from all across the globe walking many different paths of life through this community. The opportunities I had as a child to meet many people from different backgrounds are no longer "inaccessible" as anyone with a smartphone or laptop with access to the internet can have these experiences as well. Yes, meeting someone in person is a completely different experience than only meeting someone online. However, meeting someone online is also completely different, and perhaps better, than never meeting that type of person at all. I do not think that my fellow Gen Z would have a dilemma with their cultural identity because they joined so many different internet communities.

There are many advantages and disadvantages to the internet for my generation in the matter of socialization. Connecting with people has never been more convenient as everything feels like it is one tap away. Due to getting used to this convenience, finding time to connect in more meaningful ways has been harder. It is easier to catch up with someone by watching their Facebook posts or Instagram stories than to find time to meet up and talk about our days in this busy day and age.

4. CONCLUSION

I faced many struggles as a Gen Z Tsinoy who spent a significant time of my childhood in America, and coming back to spend my adolescent years in the Philippines. Given that, there are four takeaways I would like to share. The first key takeaway is the importance of language. I struggled in learning languages. Regular use is crucial in successfully becoming fluent in both comprehension and communication. Besides English, finding opportunities to practice Minnanhua and Filipino was sparse during my stay in America which resulted in me having low proficiency in those two languages when I first came back to the Philippines. With the advent of the internet, the world is becoming a much more intertwined and interconnected place. Language is a very important part of forming connections. Without Minnanhua, I would not have been able to connect with my extended Chinese family members, especially my grandmothers. Without Filipino, I would not have been able to connect with my peers as well as I would now. The second key takeaway is adjusting to new environments takes time. No big change happens overnight. It is overwhelming to take in everything all at once. Adapting to change should happen one small step at a time. The third takeaway is that sometimes a place to belong or a connection with others can be found in the least expected places and people. The place of "belonging" one is searching can sometimes be found where one is not looking. The people whom one wants to connect with may be the people who are the most different from themselves. The last takeaway is adapting to technology. The digitalization of everything is almost inevitable. The pandemic advanced the progress of this technology exponentially. It is simply a matter of how to make the most out of the new environment.

Investing Across Generations: a Personal Reflection

Josephine Tan

The journey to meeting Christ and growing in Him calls for the influence and aid of those around us. These are people we may or may not personally know who have met Christ and seen His faithfulness through the years. This is just how it works. According to a famous proverb, "It takes a village to raise a child." Our upbringing influences our decisions in life the same way our education does. The peers we choose may impact our course of actions. Even as we grow older, our colleagues at work may also affect our views, especially if we spend a lot of time with them. This fact leads me to reflect again on how having a mentor in Christ is a significant blessing. I would liken mentors to a key to the door of the gospel. Through their investment in our lives, we have access to the Word of God that in turn leads us to the grace of salvation and provides us with wisdom to live by, the only set of instructions we will ever need. When we finally experience the Truth of Christ, we know this is the ultimate authority as to how we move and live. We also have hope that even when we face trials on earth, it all does not end here. Christ has overcome it all. We hold on to promises like that in John 16:3, "I have told you these things, so that in me you may have peace. In this world you will have trouble. But take heart! I have overcome the world." We hold on to the promise of Heaven. This is especially true in my life. Over the years, I have met countless people that God used to mold me to be more and more Christlike, and He is, beyond any doubt, not finished with me yet.

In my case, looking back to when I was just seven, it took the time and effort of a selfless couple to turn me to the Truth. They are a minister couple who raised a wonderful family, one composed of individuals who dedicated their lives to being God's instruments for others to turn to Him. They served God through preaching, showing the Jesus film, music, and endeavors of charity. I have seen this family get tested in life, yet they still declare of constantly experiencing God's unfailing love in highs and lows. I talk so highly about their faith because I have witnessed them cry out to God in praise during the wee hours of the night, in the midst of battling a series of uncontrollable events, but they were never even shaken. They were eager to tell of the truth, healing, and faithfulness of God anytime and anywhere. They still ministered to my family both in season and out of season. I am grateful to have known them, and I have learned from their experience.

To this day, there are still times I recall them when I pass through another tough situation. God was and is still faithful. He was with them. He is with me. He is always faithful. Over and over again, I get to taste and see the goodness of God. With this declaration of praise, I would like to put stress on how knowing Christ deep in our heart is also significant for us in encouraging others into the Christian faith and spiritual growth, even though God can also use anyone or anything. He is God, after all. As for me, I know He will use me in season or out of season to fulfill His mission. This is a substantial lesson I learned from this couple. I am excited to share how I met this couple whom I consider my initial spiritual parents.

A MILLENIAL FROM THE PHILIPPINES

My name is Josephine Tan. I go by Jojo. I am a female and an alumna of Asia-Pacific Nazarene Theological Seminary, where I received my Master of Science in Theology in Biblical Studies. I am originally from the beautiful province of Leyte, an island in the Philippines. I have the privilege of belonging to the millennial generation. I say 'privilege' because there are advantages to being in my generation, such as being able to experience more advanced and convenient means of getting things done.

As a millennial, my parents and I had a major generational gap. They raised us in the same way they were brought up. They raised us well. They were both exceptionally hardworking. I could not ask for better parents. If there was one value that I learned from them which stood out to me, it would be humility. They taught it to us and lived by it. My late father grew up in a Chinese-influenced family. He was silent most of the time. Only when we misbehaved would his toughness come out. He used physical ways to discipline us. One thing I recall about my father, though, is that music was his love. He used to listen to classic Sunday songs. Other than that, he was mostly silent.

My mother grew up in a remote coastal area of the province, then spent most of her teenage years in a mountainous area, so she had more traditional ways of doing things. She devoted herself to gardening, farming, and livestock. Since she had grown up that way, she was the breadwinner of our family. She was not with us most of the time. Faith-wise, my parents had a generic understanding of Catholicism. I learned about basic prayer from them, but they were not Christians. As a millennial, having little interaction with my parents played a crucial role in my identity search.

To me, being a millennial is like standing on the edge of a chasm; one side is where most conservative people stand, while on the other side, I find those that boldly speak about and beg for acknowledgement of their feelings. This results in an identity crisis. I would probably have questioned my existence. It was as if Millennials walked so that Gen Zs could run.

The good thing is that I have a church family. Honestly, I have to admit that I could have searched for answers in the wrong places had I not met my spiritual parents and church friends at the early age of seven. I would have struggled through an extreme identity crisis all my teenage life had I not known my real identity in Christ. If I had had less church exposure, I probably would have done things I could never imagine doing to this day.

I am going to point out a core memory that would distinguish me as a millennial. During my teenage years, the emo/punk genre of music was on the rise. Since music played a very crucial role in coping with the identity crisis back then, young boys played emo. Young teenage girls also considered themselves as emo or else fantasized as princess characters in a Taylor Swift song. I believe most millennials can probably agree. I recall the emo side bangs, a miserable kind of look, with metal rocker-inspired fashion trends--emotion-centered music and fashion. My understanding of emo is that you feel emotional and miserable about life, but you prefer to just keep it inside or dismiss yourself. To me, it was also closely related to rebellion. This makes sense to me now since it was a period of transitioning to Gen Z, who are definitely sure about their identity and feel themselves entitled to their identity preferences. I don't know how it happened, but now, teenagers can identify as anyone or anything. Gen Zs also prefer not to be put under any inconvenience.

THE EMERGENCE OF INTERNET TECHNOLOGY

However, those emo/punk styles were the standard or influence during my teenage days. Then there was Friendster. Everyone in my class was caught up in the excitement of creating a social media account. Then we were introduced to Facebook. The idea that you could select people to accept as friends so they could see how your life was going was so new to us back then. The Kdrama marathon also started. We felt that we had to buy the CDs and watch the entire series in one sitting lasting for days. Streaming apps did not yet exist then for Kdramas.

So, I recall that we had some western emo wannabes and some Kdrama-inspired individuals. It was a generation transitioning from the old keypad cell phones to touchscreen smartphones. With the introduction of smartphones with cameras and the ability to go online, we became more active Facebook and Instagram netizens. And then, well, a lot just happened from then on. Now, my niece, as young as she is, is already familiar with Kpop idols. When I spend time with my Gen Z acquaintances, the truth of the gap daunts me even more. These are kids who can point out their feelings and would like to be appreciated and acknowledged for it. These are the moments I realize that a lot has really changed and will only keep changing.

That is when I thank God for the two wonderful people from my childhood. Without the help of this couple that I consider to be my spiritual parents, my grip on my faith and my standards would have been too fragile. I could easily have caved in to the wrong way, even to the point that I would have succumbed to actions harmful to me.

THE BEGINNING OF CHURCH LIFE

I am grateful to God that being around church, especially having spiritual second parents helped me understand who I am and where I belong. I met my spiritual parents through the help of my sister who was abroad. My sister and her husband met a minister at an event. Exchanging emails over wired internet, they were able to ask pastor Bado (not his real name) and his wife, Pastora Ry, to visit us in our town. I was only seven years old at the time. They lived an hour away. They had to take a bus to reach our location. They did this for months until we also started making bus trips to their church every Sunday morning, and then they drove us home and conducted Bible studies in the afternoon after church. I had enthusiastic Sunday School teachers who were always creative in presenting children's Bible stories. I recall being excited to attend Sunday school for games and prizes.

Our home-based Bible studies eventually grew bigger. When I reached high school, we were already holding a children's ministry, which continued until I graduated. A lot has changed since then. Pastor Bado has already left this life. My Sunday school teachers are all married now. I cannot recall all the children we ministered to anymore, but one thing is certain: all these people and ministries solidified my faith and goals in life. It is a core memory I always love to look back. I am always grateful to my mentors.

The efforts my spiritual parents gave to build my family's faith were remarkable. I recall a family event that was unexpected, and they allowed us to stay in their home even though they were also going through a difficult time. The demonstrations of their faith are still very vivid to me. Instead of complaining at dawn, they cried out in praise to God. I saw Christ in them. I can only pray that I will have that kind of influence too. My childhood was not the most ideal, but when they entered our lives, they consistently devoted themselves to helping my siblings and me in our spiritual growth.

A FUTURE PLACED IN FAITH

When I graduated from high school, I stopped studying for two years to help a relative run her preschool which was in its first years of operation. During this time, I was reflecting really hard on my future. Then God led me back to Himself, and I began to pursue my love for biblical history. Since I was young, I always had a fascination about what really happened back then in the children's Bible stories, how they communicated, and what their world really looked like. When I answered this call to do Biblical Studies, I found not only my curiosity being satisfied by learning the biblical context, but my faith growing even deeper as well. I found myself in awe of how God can actually use any generation to perform His wonders. He qualified the unqualified. He can use anyone, anything, and any circumstance. He is still doing it through us. Growing in intimacy with Christ, I can attest to His faithfulness up to this day. My love for biblical Hebrew led me to be a teacher. I received the opportunity to teach basic biblical

Hebrew in a Bible college in Benguet (Philippines), where I interact with student ministers and religious teachers.

Without intimacy with Christ, I could not teach passionately. It takes a heart fully surrendered to his will, and a heart after God's own heart. I emphasize knowing God deep in our heart because we can't give what we do not have. If we have not fully encountered Christ, God cannot fully use us, our talents, or our resources for the expansion of His kingdom. God is still molding me into Christlikeness. I am grateful that God used people to plant a seed in me so that, no matter the changing time, I know who I am, and I am certain of my purpose.

MILLENIALS AND GEN Z

Generational gaps are a serious issue. Moreover, they are becoming even wider. There is already a delulu as a solulu mindset. These are slang terms that mean that as long as you believe it in your mind, then it is the truth. Another new concept is the power of manifesting. If you manifest it, it is likely to happen. Some of the newer Gen Zs have already taken this "I identify as" agenda and LGBTQA+++ advocacy a little too far. They believe that what they believe is the truth, and they will stand for it. By standing for it, they are willing to resort to fights and even more intense actions. When we try to call these out, we incur a lot of hate. Everyone in these generations is starting to become too sensitive. It seems that every topic has become too sensitive to point out and discuss. But when we know the truth, we are compelled to let it be known because, otherwise, who will do it? It is not an easy undertaking. It is getting even more challenging. The harvest continues to rise in number while the workers remain few. With the rise of so many ideologies, the Truth gets concealed a little more. A lot of what used to be unacceptable has already become a normal thing. I recall John Wesley's words, "What one generation tolerates, the next generation will embrace." They need me. They need you. They need us. If my mentors, especially Pastora Ry, practiced consistency, it just goes to show that Kingdom work requires a lot more than just sharing--it calls for constant effort to remind the generation around us of their identity in Christ.

It takes those who know Christ to plant the seeds and invest in those who need help in their spiritual growth. Investing in someone's spiritual growth requires us to give our time and our resources. We give all we can, whether in season or out of season. This is what we live for.

He Remains Faithful: Reflections of a Baby Boomer

*Alice Wulbern**

It was the summer of 1978. I was sitting in a weekend missions conference at my church in North Carolina. A missionary to Mexico was the speaker, and he was challenging us to respond to Jesus' command to "Go and make disciples of all nations." A thought popped into my head: China has about 20% of the world's population, so if China can be evangelized, that will take care of a big chunk of fulfilling the Great Commission.

At the time, I was 27, married for one year, and working as a symphony orchestra musician and private music teacher. Typical of a Baby Boomer growing up in the southern United States, I had regularly attended church as a child. I put my faith in Christ while in primary school but then, as a college student, had questioned my faith. As soon as I resolved my intellectual doubts, I ran up against self-doubts—that is, my inability to live a Christian life. The temptations and allurement of a worldly life seemed all too strong. For me, the answer came in the form of an encounter with the Holy Spirit which changed my Christian walk from a burdensome duty to a treasured relationship. As I continued along my career path in music, I also dove into Bible study and prayer groups, local ministry, and a deepening awareness that every Christian is called to serve God, whether in lay ministry or professional service. This all took place in the 1970s milieu of the Jesus People Movement and Charismatic Renewal. Many churches, families, and Baby Boomer individuals were profoundly influenced by this period of spiritual awakening. Much has been written in both praise and criticism of this part of American Christian history; I can only say that I know a number of dedicated, faithful, and fruitful ministries that sprang forth and grew during those years.

THE CALLING

Returning to my personal story, the months that followed that weekend missions conference brought about a total change of direction in my life. My husband, who was a junior high school science teacher, was asked to serve on the missions committee of our church. So, when he was invited to accompany two other men from the church on a visit to missionaries working in southern Mexico, he gladly agreed. In fact, he knew almost nothing about missions and felt that he needed to see some real-life mission work in order to serve more knowledgeably on the missions committee. During the week that he was away, God did a deep work in each of us individually. For me, it was the voice of the Spirit convincing me that I should resign from the orchestra—but I didn't know why. For my husband, it was the experience of meeting villagers in southern Mexico hungry to know God and to learn from his Word, but with too few missionaries to fill the need. We soon made the decision to leave our home and go to Mexico, apprentice ourselves to two missionary families that were working in the state of Oaxaca, and find out if God could use us to share the gospel and make disciples.

Were we crazy? Perhaps, although I like to think that we were foolish for God. I remember talking to my father just a week or so before we left. A man who was normally quick to express his opinions, he had been unusually quiet about our decision. So, I asked him directly, "How do you feel about our going to the mission field in this way?" He answered, "I think it's interesting." I believe that, like

Gamaliel in the fifth chapter of Acts, while he was not completely convinced that what we were doing was of God, he didn't want to oppose us, in case God were to bless it.

As it turned out, we spent nine years in Oaxaca learning Spanish, learning culture, learning a variety of missions-related ministries, and putting it all into practice. Most important of all, we were learning to trust God's faithfulness. This faithfulness evidenced itself in numerous ways, too many for me to recount in this reflection. One of our first lessons, however, was about God's provision. In our first two years, our home church in the U.S. and several of the individuals that we thought we could rely on for support did not come through. Instead, God provided for us in unexpected ways and through unexpected people. One example was also a situation God used to teach me humility. Before going to Mexico, I had joined three other women from different churches in a ministry to women incarcerated in the county jail. The last Sunday that I went there, one of the women had handed me a bill, and said, "I know this isn't much, but I want you to know that I will be praying for you." I looked at the five-dollar bill, stuffed it into my shoulder bag, and thought, "Yeah, you're right. It isn't much," About five months later, when we were pinching our pesos and hoping for a check in the mail, I looked in that shoulder bag for something else and came across the five-dollar bill. I jumped up and shouted, "We have five dollars! We have five dollars!" That gift reappeared at a critical time, demonstrating God's faithful provision and teaching me not to look down on any gift given out of love for the Lord.

Another provision came the next year, when the Lord moved on the heart of the pastor of a new church in Louisiana. He read a newsletter we had sent to a friend who was a member of the church, and he talked to her and another couple who knew us. Several weeks later, seemingly out of the blue, we received a letter from Pastor Jerry, telling us that the church was going to start sending us monthly support. The church supported us for nine months before we went to the U.S. and were able to visit the church and meet Pastor Jerry for the first time. One of the greatest blessings was being introduced to the church secretary and having her say, "Oh, you're the missionaries we've been praying for every week!" In his faithfulness, the Lord connected us with a pastor and a church that became our church home and family for many years. The financial support was important, but the relationships, prayers, and ministry connections were vital and created avenues of mutual blessing.

MISSION LIFE IN LATIN AMERICA

As a young missionary, serving in evangelism, leading Bible studies, working with youth and children, I yearned to be a woman of faith, undaunted by any challenges, and I looked up to strong women like Corrie ten Boom and Catherine Marshall and Elisabeth Elliot. What I learned, however, from the Lord's demonstrations of faithfulness while serving in Mexico can be summed up in these verses from Second Timothy:

[11] The statement is trustworthy:

For if we died with Him, we will also live with Him;
[12] If we endure, we will also reign with Him;
If we deny Him, He will also deny us;
[13] If we are faithless, He remains faithful, for He cannot deny Himself. (2 Tim 2:11-13, NASB)

My faith might be weak, but God is always, always faithful to those who remain in him.

During our ninth year in Mexico, it became clear that God was leading us to leave Oaxaca. At first, we weren't sure whether we should go to another part of Mexico or to another country. From the beginning, we had felt that Mexico was to be a training ground, and we were certain that we would eventually go to Asia. However, that was not yet to be. Instead, the Lord very clearly directed us to the Mosquito Coast of Honduras—a place I knew nothing about! This was an example of another aspect of God's character and working in our lives.

As followers of Christ, we try hard to be sure that we are "in his will." When we make decisions about relationships, where to live, what kind of work to do, and other important issues, we want to be certain that we are following God's will for us. We desire the pillar of cloud by day and the pillar of fire by night to guide us everywhere we go. However, what I found in my own experience was that, while there are times that God speaks very clearly and unmistakably, there are also times that he seems to let us make our own choices from among the various options before us. Usually, his clearest leadings come when he directs us to go somewhere or do something that we wouldn't have thought of or wouldn't have wanted to do on our own.

When we were happily living and working in the U.S., it took that unmistakable voice of the Holy Spirit to move us to the mission field. Likewise, when we were considering where to go from Oaxaca, God aligned a series of "coincidences" that led us clearly to a Nicaraguan refugee camp in the jungles of Honduras. By contrast, some of our decisions had no "writing in the sky" that led us. For instance, when we had spent two years of apprenticeship in Oaxaca, we then had to choose a village or town to settle in as we moved out on our own. As much as we prayed, no unmistakable direction came to us. We felt that we should go to one of two villages, but neither one stood out to us. Finally, we made a decision, but with a feeling that our leading was 51% over 49%. Nevertheless, God blessed our work in the town of Putla over the next seven years, and in hindsight I have no doubt that he was pleased with our choice.

> *During our years in Mexico, the Lord had blessed us with three children--two adopted daughters, followed by a son who was born to me when I was 35. I was pregnant again when we moved to Honduras, and five months after arriving there, I gave birth to our third daughter. Two months later we moved to the jungle. There we lived in a rough board house with a thatch roof, no electricity, running water, or roads. As there were no phones of any kind, and this was years before the internet, we communicated by radio, which ran off a battery charged by solar panels. Snakes, bats, scorpions, and tarantulas were a normal*

> *part of life, along with bathing in a stream, cooking on kerosene burners, and sleeping under mosquito nets. That, together with our yearly income, could have caused us to think of ourselves as poor. Yet, we were the wealthy ones. The refugees we lived among cooked over wood fires and had no kerosene-powered refrigerator like we did. They relied on the UN to provide them with monthly rations of food. I learned a lot about what true wealth is when worshiping joyfully with people who had fled their country with only what they could carry on their backs, seeing their villages burning behind them. It was a powerful demonstration of Jesus' words: "Watch out! Be on your guard against all kinds of greed; life does not consist in an abundance of possessions" (Luke 12:15).*

Our time in the Mosquito Coast was spent in three villages, including Wampusirpi in the jungle, Puerto Lempira on the coast, and Cauquira on a spit of land between the Caribbean and the Laguna Caratasca. Our work with Nicaraguan refugees ended when their repatriation was completed in late 1990, but after moving to Puerto Lempira, we continued working in parachurch ministries among the Miskito people, primarily with the Moravian Church (the largest Christian group in the Mosquito Coast), but also with the Church of God and the Baptist Church. Later, in Cauquira, we also took on the administration of a medical clinic funded by the Moravian Church and the Reformed Church of America. We were joined, at different times and locations, by teammates from Mexico, including a pastor and his family, two Bible school graduates, and two doctors. My particular ministry focuses included, at various times, children's ministry, training Sunday school teachers and children's workers, leading women's Bible studies, writing and recording a children's radio program in Spanish, and directing a project for translating Sunday school materials from Spanish to Miskito.

MISSION LIFE IN CHINA

Our time in Honduras came to an end after six and a half years, due to a family crisis that required us to return to the U.S. for our first extended period in the more than fifteen years we had been on the field. As we prayed over the next year and a half, we felt certain that this was the time for us to turn our eyes towards Asia. After investigating various possibilities, the one that grabbed our hearts was in China. And so, eighteen years after the thought of China first came to my mind, we packed up our family of six and moved to the city of Changchun in the far northeast of that country.

It is hard to imagine a greater contrast than the differences between our life and ministry in the Mosquito Coast and what we encountered in Changchun. From sparsely-populated, undeveloped villages in the tropics, we moved to a dense booming city of millions not far from Siberia. We switched from missionary visas in Honduras to teachers' visas in China. We had mastered Spanish, but now we were faced with a far more difficult language. Most importantly, after working many years in traditional Christian ministries, we now took on the task of teaching English in universities where our every class and many of our other personal interactions were monitored to make sure that we were not talking about politics or religion. Students who came to visit us in our apartment on campus had to sign in with a doorman and were sometimes admonished not to "bother the teachers"—even when they were coming at our invitation.

So, once again we began the task of learning a new culture, learning a new kind of ministry, and learning enough of the language to do daily chores like shopping at the market and taking public transportation. We were blessed to be placed with experienced team mates who met with us every week and helped us to navigate the new challenges. Little by little, we gained confidence and began to share our faith in personal, relational ways. Even in my first year there, I was able to use the story of Esther in one of my classes, introducing it as a part of Persian history. The Thanksgiving, Christmas, and Easter holidays always provided opportunities to teach about "western culture." I developed lesson plans where I would teach one lesson about the historical basis of Christmas and a second lesson about the modern traditions of Christmas celebrations in the U.S. and the U.K. When reviewing the lessons, I tried to make sure that the students understood what was true historically and what was modern make-believe. This became even more important to me after I saw more than one Chinese church with cardboard pictures of Santa Clause hanging on the wall year-round. I realized to my great dismay that earlier missionaries had introduced their western traditions with as much enthusiasm as they had taught the gospel, and the result was confusion.

After four years in Changchun, we moved to a city in western China that was quite different from Changchun. There were many Muslims and many Tibetans there in addition to the majority Han Chinese. The Lord opened doors for us to make friends with several Muslim students. In order to make these friends feel more comfortable visiting us, we eliminated all pork products from our home. The Lord used me and a couple of my team mates to share God's love with one of my Muslim students. The Lord spoke to this young man's heart, and he became a fervent believer. He later went on to further studies and now works in Bible translation. In his case and in so many more, I observed firsthand the truth of Paul's words, "I planted the seed, Apollos watered it, but God has been making it grow" (1 Co 3:6).

LIFE TURNED AROUND

Around this time, I experienced a heartbreak that hurt more deeply than anything else I have ever gone through. My husband of 25 years decided to leave the ministry and me in favor of living a different kind of life. When I look back, I still think of 2006 as 'my year from hell.' And yet, in the midst of the pain and confusion and uncertainty, I received a new depth of God's faithfulness and provision. We were in the U.S. on deputation when I learned the worst, and that very week I met a woman "by chance" who had been a missionary to Japan and who had gone through a very similar experience. She gave me very valuable counsel and encouragement. We returned to

China long enough to pack things up and arrange for our replacements, then moved to the U.S. Within a few months, I was provided with a car, a place to live, and a ministry-related office job.

I was surrounded by people who cared for me and helped me. My missions leaders supported me as I received counseling and worked to establish a new life. It was clear that the Lord knew this was going to happen, and although I would never have chosen to walk this path, I could clearly see his hand of care. As I suffered the loss of my marriage and my ministry on the mission field, and as I questioned who I was and what I could do, I learned in a deeper way than ever before that "the eternal God is [my] refuge, and underneath are the everlasting arms" (Dt 33:27).

After three years in the U.S., my missions board approved me to return to China, and once again I found myself in the far northeast, this time on my own. For ten more years I taught in a Chinese university, and was blessed to be there at a time when China allowed more openness and freedom. I could see that the prayers of my friends in the U.S. were being heard. I was able to join a bilingual fellowship with Chinese as well as foreigners, unlike previous years when I could only formally worship with other foreigners. The prayers continued and the opening continued. I began to preach from time to time in the fellowship, and then was able to host two Bible studies: one for seekers (with a Chinese friend doing most of the teaching in Mandarin), and another for the leaders of the bilingual fellowship, where we took turns leading and sharing. The dedication and enthusiasm of these young adult Chinese believers was contagious, and others came to faith, including some of my college students.

Sadly, around 2018 the atmosphere of openness in China began to be shut down. Then, at the age of 67, I was told that my school could no longer extend my contract because of my age. They had kept me for two years past the usual limit of 65, but the provincial government was tightening up, so I had to go. I realized soon after that I was blessed to have a "soft" exit, with time for good-byes and no black marks on my passport. In other parts of China, including the western city where I had lived before, foreign Christians were called in by the police and given less than a week to leave the country. Then, most of those who remained left a year later because of the COVID pandemic. How important it is for us to pray for our Chinese brothers and sisters who now live in a situation that is reminiscent of the rule of Chairman Mao!

NO RETIREMENT IN MISSIONS

The Chinese government thought I should retire; in the U.S., I was eligible to retire; but I wasn't ready to retire. After several months of prayer and counsel, I went to the Philippines to teach English at the Asia-Pacific Nazarene Theological Seminary. This was an assignment wonderfully suited to my missions experiences, my disposition, and even my age. Students there come from all over Asia and, indeed, from all over the world. I taught those whose English wasn't at a high enough level for seminary studies. It was exciting to teach English to current and future ministry leaders from Korea, Myanmar, India, Africa, China, and Indonesia, as well as the Philippines. When the pandemic struck and lockdowns were imposed, classes moved online and the enrollment expanded to include students who were staying in their home countries. As a Baby Boomer, I was most certainly not a digital native, but teaching on Zoom was just another step in the increasing use of technology in the classroom—I had come a long way from my days in the Mosquito Coast!

When in-person classes were reopened and international travel began again, many of these remote students wanted to continue their studies online because of ministry and family obligations. The seminary, like many schools around the world, used what were necessary adjustments in the pandemic to extend the opportunities for studying online.

When the pandemic was ending, my time in the Philippines was also coming to an end. My missions support had been sufficient for my situation in China, but was not adequate for me to remain in the Philippines. After three years at the seminary, I moved back to the U.S. and now live near three of my four children, and also my granddaughters. But when I look at the Bible, the only person I can find who chose to retire was King David—and his retirement seems to have been the result of ill health and political necessity. One person suggested that I might look for a part-time job as a receptionist to keep busy, meet people, and have some extra income. For me, however, a Baby Boomer missionary, ministry to people of other nations is still my calling. I have continued to teach one class online for the seminary in the Philippines and I also tutor a couple of students from Myanmar online. Locally, I joined a weekly outreach to internationals, especially university students who come from other countries. Through that ministry I learned about an intensive English school for foreigners, and now I teach part-time at the school, with students from Brazil and other South American countries, Africa, China, and Korea. Some of the students are Christians, while others are not. We teachers are encouraged to share the love of God with our students. I am enjoying my "retirement". When I could no longer go to the mission field, the mission field came to me.

In summary, the Lord has been good. I could share about many more wonderful experiences and a number of other awful times, but through all of them, the Lord has been faithful. He has provided for my needs, he has guided me, he has saved souls and raised up leaders, he has comforted me in times of suffering and healed me of various diseases. He is my God and I will praise him.

> *10 He says, "Be still, and know that I am God;*
> *I will be exalted among the nations,*
> *I will be exalted in the earth."*
>
> *11 The Lord Almighty is with us;*
> *the God of Jacob is our fortress. (Ps 46:10-11)*

*Name has been changed for security reason.

Family Tragedy to Triumph: Pursuit of a Diaspora Eurasian (an Interview With Nonagenarian)

Alma Pinno Kisser

Editor's Note: This is a story of Alma, drawn from interviewing her.

Alma Pinno Kisser is a "nonagenarian" (92 years old), belonging to the so called "Silent Generation" born between 1928 and 1946. They are a generation of people called "Traditionalists." They number approximately 55 million worldwide, and are comprised of people who either fought during World War II or were children during that period..

My name is Alma Pinno Kisser, 92 years old, a widow and have been living in an independent seniors' home for almost 18 years now. I am also a volunteer at the Shepherds Care Home where I live. Currently, I attend a regular weekly Bible study. Many people in the Senior Home tell me that I am kind, welcoming, and caring. I am a mother of two children and grandmother to four grandchildren.

ANCESTRY AND TRIALS OF LIFE

My parents were Gotlieb and Olga Pinno, they were of German descent and migrated to Volhynia in Eastern Poland during the unbearable conditions in Germany. Life in Volhynia during that time was difficult. My parents farmed for their sustenance. When World War 1 broke out in August 1914, my father was drafted into the Russian Army and then became a prisoner of war. He was reunited with his family after some time.

They told me a very sad story of something that had happened earlier, before I was born: There was a time that my mother needed to work on the farm, and she had to take her children with her while leaving at home her third child, who was two years old. Because of his struggle not to be left behind, my mom tied him to the leg of the table. When they came home after work, she was shocked to find him dead, strangled with the string that had tied his neck. She felt so guilty for what she did but recovered later after she came to know the Lord personally and experienced God's forgiveness and love. Although this happened before I was born, this story made an impact in my life, producing godly fear.

My parents came to know the Lord thru the Baptist Church. Being discipled, they remained resilient through their faith in God, especially during their wartime experiences.

In 1932, my parents welcomed me, their eighth child. At first, they thought I was stillborn, as I was frail and was not responding at all upon delivery. But, according to my parents, my mom cried out and prayed fervently until the Lord touched me. I was then able to respond. That resulted in joy and thanksgiving to the Lord Almighty.

My childhood life was a struggle because of my health, but by God's grace, I overcame.

When I was seven years old, the Soviet War broke out, which led into World War II, 1939 to 1945. As a child I witnessed and suffered the following:

- I experienced the rule of the Nazi empire with all its pain and horrors.
- We were moved from camp to camp, experiencing fear, exhaustion, and sickness. I experienced "frozen foot" that still affects me even now. My father and brothers were drafted into the army, leaving us only with mom.
- I saw oppression that included Jews being taken away from the neighborhood.
- We could not go to church, but our parents would attend worship and prayer in secret. The churches were used as granaries.
- I heard many horrifying stories. We were also in hiding.
- We did not have enough food to eat, but even so, my mom still shared food with others who were suffering from hunger.

But God intervened in all of these sufferings. My mom always prayed, trusting God and giving thanks even there was no food, and God would provide food in an amazing way. One time, a Polish soldier herded us all together as a family and prepared to shoot and kill us, but then a Russian soldier came to rescue us. He was used by God to save us.

During the war, we went through a lot of hardships in living without our father and other brothers, as they were on the battlefield. One of my brothers died in the war. This was painful for us. We struggled through other humiliations and horrors, including the delousing of all women, the rape of our neighbors, the persecution of Christians, failures, sickness, hunger, pain, and more.

And yet, these were used by God to open my eyes to life's difficulties. I realized my need of supernatural power to go on, and it led me to seek God. I witnessed and received the love of God, saving us and providing for our needs. There is a God who is alive. This realization developed my faith. My character of helping people also developed, as I emulated my parents, especially my mom.

LIFE AFTER THE WAR

After the war, we moved to another place and joined a local church. Later, my parents started a prayer group in our home. I liked the pastor teaching and praying for us. When I turned 15 years old, I loved attending the youth group. In one of the services, when the pastor gave an altar call, I went forward and prayed to receive Jesus as my Lord and Savior. Since that day, I have always been drawn to worship God and to know Him. I have continued to be drawn to study the Bible and attend church services. Even now, at 92 years old, I faithfully attend Bible study, visit patients, and volunteer in our local church and our senior's home events. My goal is always to know, love, and serve God in words and in deeds.

A few years after the war, I desired a better place to live. Germany at that time was divided into East and West, and East Germany was under Communism. After consultation and praying with the family, they blessed me to find a better life in another country where my two brothers had immigrated earlier. In 1951, at the age of 19, I sailed to Canada with other Germans. Arriving there, I met Walter, a fellow German and friend of my brother. We dated and then got married in 1955. We finally settled in Edmonton where we became very involved in church. We had difficulties at first, but soon we were established and lived a better and more peaceful life in spite of various health challenges.

In life's difficulties, I always look for a spiritual family, a church where we can be anchored. The church has always been a support to our family, especially in times of trials, sickness and need. Wherever we moved, we always found a church to join and would serve God volunteering in their programs and visiting the weak and sick. We became established in Edmonton later, so we are with our two children and now grandchildren, too. These days, although I am already 92, assisted by a walker to be able to move around, I still go to church and volunteer.

EDITOR'S CONCLUSION

Alma is like a tree planted along the riverbank, bearing fruit in each season, whose leaves never wither, and prospering in all she does because her delight is in God, meditating on His words, and following Him (see Psalms 1:4).

The following factors have contributed to her seeking and following God:

1) Trials and sufferings

Alma's experience of trials and sufferings while growing up during the war encouraged her to seek and follow God. These contributed to her resilience and enduring power. In spite of her physical health problems, she is still enjoying emotional and mental health in her senior years. Although she was born weak and almost died in her early years in Canada, she has reached 92 years old.

2) Godly family heritage

Alma and her siblings were taught about God. Her parents were strict but loving and prayerful. They taught their children the importance of both attending and being involved in a local church.

When challenges came to them like hunger and the horrors of war, the parents modeled the practice of prayer, trusting God and thanking Him even for small needs and difficulties. Alma's mother stayed with them, sharing with them that there is a loving God and He is at work. She also instructed them and modelled for them the importance of hard work, compassion, kindness, and strong faith.

3) Bible believing and practicing local church

The family always looked for a local church, a spiritual family, and support. The church stood with them in good times and bad times.

4) Absence of Technology

The absence or scarcity of many technological entertainments like TV, internet, cellphones, and video games allowed them time for work, family interaction, church activities, and playtime with friends, encouraging good family relationships, and social and work time spent together with others.

Today, generations are changing.

They are characterized by busyness, less time to be with the kids, not being able to teach good manners and right conduct, inability to teach about God, to be responsible, and other godly values. Because of less or no experience of trials and sufferings, they are easily affected and have become sensitive, easily discouraged, depressed, and sometimes suicidal.

Much of the teachings now is through technology like the internet. The internet, along with TV, video games, social media, etc., steal important time. It is easier now to just "attend" church at home with online streaming, eliminating time spent in fellowship to encourage each other.

How should we reach the existing octogenarians, nonagenarians, including the seniors living in retirement homes and in assisted living? I never saw this as a ministry until my wife and I needed to live in a seniors' home because I had had a stroke and needed assistance. Our seniors home became our added mission field. Here we see people suffering all around. They are here living with us! So, now we visit and pray for them, lead Bible studies, and encourage and cheer them. Even—maybe especially--the very old need Jesus! They need practical demonstrations of His love and presence, and even Christian seniors need encouragement and fellowship as they often face loneliness and are unable to attend church services. This is indeed an open field for missions and ministry.

The Centenarian: Receiving Their Personal Legacy

Sadiri Joy Tira

ESTHER CORTADO BRIONES – TIRA

She was born July 1st, 1924 in a remote town of Pagadian, Zamboanga, Philippines. Her parents, Perpetua Cortado and Aquilino Briones, were Methodist Missionaries to the southern island Mindanao, Philippines.

Esther was married to Victorino Bergonia Tira of Urdaneta, Pangasinan, Luzon Island of the Philippines. He was born on December 5, 1919. Together, they raised six godly children. Their 5th child is Sadiri "Joy" Emmanuel Santiago.

Every time I visit Manila, I visited their graves in the cemetery to give thanks to God for the legacy of my parents. They were school teachers and land owners in Mindanao. They taught me how to read and write. They regularly brought me to the church. They introduced me to Jesus Christ. They prayed that like their parents, Aquilino and Perpetua, I would someday become a missionary and pastor. When I was born, they dedicated me to God and to serve the Kingdom. Their prayers were answered!

My Dad modelled frugality and a simple life style. He emphasized the need to respect others and be generous to the needy, especially the fatherless and the orphaned. My parents adopted these orphans and poor children. My mother taught me to pray three times a day and to thank God for every meal. And at the age of five, she taught me this missional song:

Jesus loves the little children,
All the children of the world,
red, brown, yellow, black and white,
They are precious in His sight
Jesus loves the little children of the world

I grew up singing this song and passed on to my two children when they were young!

When I graduated from high school to enter the first year as university student; my parents gave me my first copy of the Bible (Living Bible). Before leaving our home, my mother and father read to me Psalm 1:1-6:

Oh the joys of those who do not follow the advice of the wicked or stand around with sinners or join in with mockers.

But they delight in the law of the Lord meditating it day and night

They are like trees planted along the riverbank bearing fruit each season. The leaves never wither and they prosper in all they do.

But not the wicked. They are like worthless chaff scattered by the wind. They will be condemned at the time of judgment. Sinners will have no place among the godly;

For the Lord watches over the path of the godly but the path of the wicked leads to destruction.

I must confess that during my high school days I was defiant and disobeyed my parents, specifically my mother's instructions. It brought them pain, but they never stopped praying for me. My father reminded me that mother asked for me from God. They dedicated me to the Lord. Like Samuel, I was God-given to her in answer to her earnest prayer (compare 1 Samuel 1:20).

Godly mothers have key roles in Generational Missiology. Imagine how Jochebed, the mother of Moses, cared for her son in her womb during the most difficult days of the Hebrews. Mary, the mother of Jesus did not abort him when she was in her womb. Both Jochebed and Mary, were Pro-life women. Inter-generational mission starts at home.

This year my mother would have turned 100 years old, a Centenarian woman. And her legacy remains! She introduced me to Jesus and taught me that He loves all the children of the world. She also loved my girlfriend (who would later became my wife!).

My father gave me and my son each a copy of his Bibles. He prayed that his grandson would become a pastor; his prayer was answered! My son is now a pastor. Silver and gold or fancy cars, boats, and a huge mansion he did not give his son and grandson! But he gave us the written-printed Word of the Lord.

Generational missiology must live long beyond 21st century and beyond, but only with the recipients of their Christian forerunners' legacy. They must be moored to the Word and introduce Jesus as Saviour and Lord among their peers and the people around them.

IV.
Pastoral Exhortation

Intergenerational Mission: Passing Our Faith Legacy to the Next Generations

Rosa C. Shao

INTRODUCTION

This past Christmas, my husband, Joseph, celebrated his 70th birthday. Our children kept asking, "Dad, what gift would you like for your birthday? Tell us!" We have never been keen on celebrating birthdays, but since a 70th festive birthday is quite a milestone, our children wanted it to be truly special for their dad.

Honestly speaking, as we enter our senior years, we no longer have a desire for more material things. Instead, we have started to declutter and downsize, trying to reduce our material belongings to the basic needs of life. Although we ourselves are quickly moving into our twilight years, we continue to learn from many God-fearing seniors still active in God's kingdom ministry during their later years.

We see them fighting the good fight, tirelessly and incessantly, till their last breath. People like John Stott, who found energy to impart God's truth to his group of brilliant students, as well as spend leisure time doing bird watching. Or, the respected Bible scholar, teacher and preacher, Tim Keller, who battled serious cancer under God's grace. When his death was imminent, he gathered his loved ones in his room and bid them a joyful and faithful farewell, exclaiming, "I am going home to see Jesus! I can't wait!"

Nonetheless, a 70th birthday celebration with family members and close friends still calls for treats and gifts to send and receive. But, if there is one desire in our hearts that we truly want, it is that "I have no greater joy than to hear that my children are walking (following) the truth" (3 John 4). This has been our fervent wish, even as we move into roles as grandparents with six grandchildren between our three adult children and their spouses, and parenting tasks to learn and re-learn.

When COVID-19 forced the world into lockdown in March 2020, we were quarantining in California, but were able to welcome the birth of our third and fourth grandchildren (in California and Ohio, respectively). During this time God, in his marvelous wisdom and divine guidance, transformed our local retirement after over 30 years of theological and pastoral ministries in the Philippines, to our glocal re-assignment in the United States where we are now continuing our theological teaching and life coaching to students from various parts of the globe. With the families of each of our three adult children all residing in the U.S., we feel a strategic call for intentional intergenerational mission to pass our faith on to the next generations.

I. UNDERSTANDING BASIC RELATIONSHIP CONCEPTS

No man is an island as the global world becomes more and more interconnected. It seems when one nation catches a cold, other countries near and far also sneeze! We read this truth about mankind in relationship from "in the beginning," when God said, "Let us make man in our image and in our likeness" (Gen. 1: 26-27). The Bible states that mankind, meaning us, is made in the image of God (imago deo). Thus, humans, like God, are not only living, but also created to be in relationship. The Bible later reveals that God himself is the triune God, three persons sharing one divine essence.

It has been said that relationships are always hierarchical, that is, a relationship defines a many-to-one relationship between two entities. From God's creation, we learn that there is the Creator-creature relationship, wherein created beings are under the reign of the Creator. Another unit can be referred to as the parent entity and the child entity. There can also be generational relationships between grandparents and grandchildren, or relationships between siblings based on birth order.

A. INTERGENERATIONAL RELATIONSHIPS

From Merriam-Webster's dictionary, the term intergenerational is an adjective, which means "existing or occurring between generations." In other words, it is "involving different generations." As such, we see the coming together of different aged groups, representing different generations, and affecting one another. The Chinese word for such phenomenon in parenting is known as 隔代教養 (ge-dai-jiao-yang). It means to do parenting tasks across generations, such as between grandparents and grandchildren.

Another related term is multi-generational. Multi-generational households are defined as including two or more adult generations (with adults generally aged 25 or older) or a skipped generation, which consists of grandparents and their grandchildren younger than 25. Most multi-generational households consist of at least two adult generations – for example, young adults living with their parents, parents residing in their adult children's homes, or a grandparent, adult child and adult grandchild together under one roof. About 5% of multi-generational households consist of grandparents and grandchildren younger than 25.[97]

The number of people who live in multi-generational family households is larger today than it was in the 1970s. In fact, the share of the U.S. population living in multi-generational homes more than doubled over the past five decades. This is partly because the groups that account for the most recent overall population growth in the U.S., including foreign-born Asian, Black and Hispanic Americans, are more likely to live with multiple generations under one roof. Another factor is the growing graying population (with the baby boomer generation as the grandparents) who may need family members to be caregivers (millennials as the adult children) because of the instability and uncertainty of the economy. On the other hand, adult children with Gen X, Y or Z children may find having grandparents as the caregivers, grannies as nannies, is the best economical and emotional setup after all.

> The many generations are now classified as follows:
> GI Generation—born 1901–1926
> Mature/Silents—born 1927–1945
> Baby Boomers—born 1946–1964
> Generation X—born 1965–1980
> Generation Y (aka Millennials)—born 1981–2000
> Generation Z (aka Boomlets or the "I" generation)—born after 2001.
> Generation Alpha (Born 2012-2025)

Generation Alpha is the name given by social analyst Mark McCrindle to the youngest children on the planet. By the year 2025, there will be nearly 2 billion members of Generation Alpha across the globe.[98]

---

[97] Pew Research Center. "The Demographics of Multigenerational Households," https://www.pewresearch.org/social-trends/2022/03/24/the-demographics-of-multigenerational-households/, accessed January 30, 2024.

[98] Kasasa. "Boomers, Gen X, GenY, Gen Z, and Gen Z Explained." Blog posted June 22, 2023, https://offer.kasasa.com/blog/boomers-gen-x-gen-y-gen-z-and-gen-a-explained,

From Womb to Tomb

B. ATTACHMENT THEORY

Attachment is a bond, emotional and affectional in nature, formed between one person and another that endures over time, and transcends space. The theory on attachment originated from the works of Bowlby and Ainsworth. John Bowlby believed that attachment was an all-or-nothing process. He believed that children come into the world biologically pre-programmed to form attachments with others, because those bonds would help them survive.[99] One of the primary paradigms in attachment theory is the security of an individual's attachment (Ainsworth and Bell, 1970). The basic assumption of this theory is that the primary caregiver (who is usually the mother), functions as a safe place where the infant can experience safety and security. The dynamics of the relationship of the infant with their primary caregiver is then internalized to form an "internal working model" of close relationships for the individual later in their life.

Psychologist Mary Ainsworth devised an assessment technique called the Strange Situation Classification (SSC) to investigate how attachments might vary between children. Through a brief 3-minute separation between mother and baby in a strange situation, three attachment styles between the two were observed. Ainsworth summarized the styles as secured, anxious-insecure, and avoidant-insecure outcomes[100]:

1. Secured: the infant is easily comforted when reunited with their mother.
2. Anxious-insecure: the infant is angry at their mother's departure due to her uncertain and unpredictable responses; the infant can be violent and question maternal love.

---

accessed January 29, 2024.
[99] Saul McLeod. "John Bowlby's Attachment Theory," https://www.simplypsychology.org/bowlby.html, accessed February 5, 2024.
[100] _____. "Mary Ainsworth: Strange Situation Experiment & Attachment Theory," https://www.simplypsychology.org/mary-ainsworth.html, accessed January 30, 2024.

3. Avoidant-insecure: the infant not only ignores the mother, but also avoids the mother's eyes, as they often feel rejected by the mother.

The quality of the bonding an infant experience during this first relationship often determines how well they relate to other people and respond to intimacy throughout life. Infants with insecure attachment often grow into adults who have difficulty understanding their own emotions and the feelings of others, limiting their ability to build or maintain stable relationships. They may find it difficult to connect to others, they may shy away from intimacy, or be too clingy, fearful, or anxious in a relationship.

Today, when we talk about attachment, we refer to a solid emotional bond between two people. Our first emotional bond is created when we are born, and we immediately seek to connect with our parents or primary caregiver. From the moment we come to this world, our brains are wired to connect with that special person who will nurture, protect, and comfort us. That primary parent-child relationship will influence future relationships we have later in adult life—especially intimate relationships. Psychologists after Bowlby and Ainsworth found that these initial attachment styles impact the way we relate, love, and seek love from others as adults.[101] These styles are:

1. **Disorganized-Insecure Attachment:** resulting from caregivers who respond to their child's needs or feelings of distress using unhealthy, violent, or neglectful ways. As an adult, a person with this attachment style, may find himself battling between wanting to be loved but engaging in negative, controlling, or neglectful behaviors toward their partner.
2. **Avoidant-Dismissive Attachment:** resulting from caregivers who dismiss the child's needs, such as leaving a child unattended when crying, failing to feed the child regularly, avoiding interacting with the child, etc. As an adult, this

---

[101] Well Beings Counselling. "The 4 Styles of Attachment," https://wellbeingscounselling.ca/the-4-styles-of-attachment/, accessed February 5, 2024.

person may be cautious or skeptical about developing intimate relationships. Deep inside, they may feel fear of rejection when opening up to another person.

3. **Anxious-Preoccupied Attachment:** resulting from caregivers being overly protective, pre-occupied, or worried about the child. The child may become clingy and agitated when their needs are not immediately met. As an adult they may feel emotionally dependent on their partner and seek continuous approval and reassurance in relationships.
4. **Secure Attachment:** resulting from caregivers being responsive to the child's signals, showing acceptance to the child's needs and being accessible to them. As an adult, this person has enough confidence to explore the world and does not feel afraid to share affection and talk about one's needs in a healthy manner. They can develop trust and are open to establish shared goals in relationships.

Knowing one's attachments style can allow for better understanding among people at home, at work and at church. It can also help in having empathy toward those who may have grown up in a challenging home environment. There is no perfect attachment, and we need to have compassion when we are around people who may be carrying traumatic experiences, known or unknown, in their consciousness. One of my friends, who is the head of an orphanage, the Bethany Children Home in Taipei, Taiwan, recounted that once she was asked to speak to a group of troubled youth. She noticed that most of them had a bent body posture, with their eyes looking down toward the table. Most of the children came from abusive parents and troubled homes. She was burdened to extend loving care and empowering attention on them. She has now gathered a group of her staff and specifically trained them to serve as parents, and even grandparents to those long-forsaken youth at the organization.[102]

---

102 Sharon To, "Practical Examples of Attachment Relationships" in *Family Series: Intentionally Christian Grandparents- Passing on Faith Through the Generations*, ed., Amy Lin (Taipei: Prue Nard Publishing House, 2023), 125 (119-133).

II. URGENCY FOR GRANDPARENTING COALITIONS

Whatever one's specific relationship problems are, it is important to know and identify one's attachment style. Then one can learn to challenge their insecurities and develop a more secure way of relating to others. Moreover, recent brain studies revealed that our brain remains capable of change as due to its plausibility throughout life. Any experiences that occur between infancy and adulthood can also impact and shape one's relationships. It is possible to re-wire one's attachment style, but this requires conscious effort. Even when one's experiences are rooted in one's brain, it takes time to replace an old habit with a new one. It takes time to replace a disorganized, anxious, or avoidant attachment style with a secure one. This is good news. A person can benefit from being surrounded with others who have secure attachment styles.

This is where grandparenting comes onto the scene. When we talk and think about generational mission, we are not only trying to reach out to different groups of people throughout the centuries, but also seeing how different groups of Christian believers can be called to live and witness their faith as they meet with either the older and/or younger generation during their lifetime.

After attending the American Grandparenting Summit for some years since 2016, a group of Chinese leaders and pastors actively and eagerly organized the Chinese Grandparenting Legacy Coalition. Seeing that it is commonplace for Chinese families to live in multi-generational housing conditions, i.e. three generations in one house, Chinese Christian grandparents may find their calling to become Jesus' witnesses in their own home. These Christian grandparents may have many opportunities to share their faith and leave a strong Christian legacy to their grandchildren and even to subsequent generations by God's grace.

A. THE COUNSEL FROM GOD'S WORD

The whole Bible, from Genesis to Revelation, gives us truth about God's covenant relationship with mankind. The phrase, "the God of Abraham, of Isaac, and of Jacob …" reveals that God is the one true living God, who initiates a precious bond with us from generation to generation (Exod. 3:15; Matt. 22:32). It is true that God's people are his children, and that God has no grandchildren. This is because every generation must find their own personal faith in the one and only true God. With the promise of the Messiah from the Old Testament, fulfilled in the birth and ministry of Jesus Christ as seen from the New Testament, the lordship and salvation in Christ is a personal matter. Every generation of descendants must make their own decision to be God's people and walk in his ways.

1. FROM GENERATION TO GENERATION

Our God desires that all people from generation to generation come to know him and praise him. When the Israelites were about to enter the Promised Land after receiving God's Ten Commandments and other instructions in daily living, God commanded Moses, saying, "Now, Israel, hear the decrees and laws I am about to teach you. Follow them so that you may live and may go in and take possession of the land the Lord, the God of your ancestors, is giving you.… Only be careful and watch yourselves closely so that you do not forget the things your eyes have seen or let them fade from your heart as long as you live. Teach them to your children and to their children after them" (Deut. 4:1-2, 9).

The Psalms is filled with exclamations, calling forth each generation, as well as future generations, to worship, adore and follow God, who is compassionate and gracious, slow to anger, abounding in love. From everlasting to everlasting, the Lord's love is with those who fear him, and his righteousness with their children's children

(Ps. 103:8, 17-18; 119:90). For God's people to praise Him from generation to generation, each generation must tell their children of God's mighty works and proclaim God's wondrous power that continues to happen in their lives (Ps. 79:13; 145:4). As every generation tells their children, the next generation is being prepared to follow God's plan for their lives.

Even after the fall of mankind, God still manifests his mercy and justice in the world. In every generation, God continues to seek people who desire him, trust him, and obey his Word. God established a home for them, just as he said to Moses, "For I, the Lord your God, am a jealous God, visiting the sin of the fathers on the children to the third and fourth generation of those who hate me; I will show lovingkindness to a thousand generations of those who love me and keep my commandments" (Exod. 20:5-6). God values his relationship with us; that relationship also concerns our descendants.

There are about 166 records of generations, that is, family history, in the Bible. I am trying to record scriptural passages whenever I encounter the word generation during my daily quiet time. Frankly, I am still counting and writing them down. It is noted that there are 51 verses referencing the phrase generation to generation.

2. TEACHINGS IN PSALM 71

Are we as grandparents too old to fight for our next generation? One psalmist in the Bible proclaimed his personal encounters with God, testifying how God is mighty to save him as he continued to trust and hope in God since birth. Psalm 71 was written by someone who was likely an old man. In his aging years, he asserted how God had been his refuge as he experienced many trials and problems throughout his life. The psalmist is affirming with confidence and acknowledging with grace that God remained righteous and faithful throughout his whole life.

How can we grow old gracefully? The lifespan of mankind has increased due to healthier living and better nutrition. Some people claim that life starts at 60, since we see many elderly living to 100! Nevertheless, growing old can be frightening and challenging. As we become grandparents, we may become less strong and sometimes even feel useless, especially after retirement.

The elderly may feel lonely, depressed, and have difficulty socializing. They may feel alienated from children and grandchildren who are busy with other interests and pursuits. This is inevitable, but as Christian grandparents we must cheer up because aging is a compulsory course for everyone! Thinking about the issue of old age is not only important for the elderly, but also a subject that everyone should pay attention to. By facing the aging process, we can have a successful life and understand the secret of survival.

There are many verses in the Bible that remind and challenge Christian grandparents to pay attention to God's mission of passing on our faith to our descendants. As we get older, we have more experiences from a genuine relationship with God that strengthen our faith. We must learn from the psalmist who continues to hold on to his initial trust as he grows older and sings to the Lord, both day and night. Not only can we grow old gracefully, but we must also let our children and grandchildren see God's love, for His faithfulness is everlasting.[103]

(A) ACKNOWLEDGING GOD'S SOVEREIGNTY IN LIFE (PS. 71:5, 6)

With great confidence in God, the psalmist declared, "For you have been my hope, Sovereign Lord, my confidence since my youth. From birth I have relied on you; you brought me forth from my mother's womb. I will ever praise you."

An old saying states, "Memory is a gift from the old." As seniors, we can observe and reflect on how the Lord has led us through high mountains and low valleys in our life. We should be willing to trust and obey, to accept everything! As we recognize our Benefactor and accept the Lord's sovereignty, we will not be afraid of growing old!

---

[103] Rosa C. Shao, "Rethinking the Faith Legacy" in *Family Series: Intentionally Christian Grandparents- Passing on Faith Through the Generations*, ed., Amy Lin (Taipei: Pure Nard Publishing House, 2023), 106-109 (90-118).

Additionally, accepting our circumstances may reduce the sadness of growing old.

(B) ADORING GOD'S DEEDS WITH OUR LIPS (PS. 71:14, 23)

The psalmist did not stop praising God. He had experienced the nearness of God who helped save him from howling enemies when he cried out to God. Thus, his hope in God grew stronger, even as he pronounced, "But I will always hope; I will praise you more and more." The Christian life is a life of singing praises to the Benefactor. A believer who knows how to sing praises to the Lord will be happy and stable in body, mind, and soul. Remembering the price of our Savior Jesus' atonement for our sins and the hope and assurance of eternal life in the Lord can make our hearts sing with joy. No wonder the psalmist said, "When I sing your praises, my lips and my soul, which you have redeemed me, will sing for joy."

(3) PROCLAIMING GOD'S POWER TO THE NEXT GENERATION (PS. 71:17-18)

The psalmist looked ahead to future generations, sharing the power of God as he beseeched the Lord to never leave him. He confirmed his desire to witness for God, declaring, "Since my youth, O God, you have taught me and to this day I declare your marvelous deeds. Even when I am old and gray, do not forsake me, O God, till I declare your power to the next generations, your mighty acts to all who are to come." Christian grandparents have a great task even in their graying years—to witness to their children and grandchildren the presence and power of the Lord in their life. This is their missionary mandate, which is to share and pass on to the future generation the most important wisdom in life: to fear God and live for his glory.

When I shared this message to 50-60 attendees at a zoom gathering at Evergreen Fellowship, I noticed that their average age was around 70. Almost everyone was retirement age. Group discussion and sharing time followed my message. One elderly woman shared that she deliberately required that her children and grandchildren take turns accompanying her to the church for fellowship, prayer meetings and worship every week. When she was 71 years old, an old illness relapsed. She couldn't buy Chinese medicine at that time, so she asked God, "What should I do?" Her old illness was cured by memorizing the Bible and singing hymns! She often said to her grandchildren, "Although I am old, my memory is failing, and I have high blood pressure, I still continue to memorize the Bible. I pray, and praise, and nourish my body, mind, and spirit with God's words." What a brilliant and beautiful way to pass on to her descendants her trust in God's mighty Word in times of need.

A. THE CALL FOR INTENTIONAL GRANDPARENTING

As if it was only yesterday, I vividly recall the years when my husband, Joseph, and I, served at the Biblical Seminary of the Philippines. Each school year, groups of Chinese students came, eager to be equipped through theological training and to prepare themselves to serve the Lord. More than 80% of the freshmen came from the Big Country in Asia. Every new student submitted their testimony as part of the application process. At the start of the school year, we usually had a special meeting to greet and get to know new students and help them feel welcome.

From their testimonies, the students' spiritual journeys and growing faith revealed different struggles. However, many testimonies shared one vital element, the influence of a God-fearing grandmother who provided spiritual teaching and a godly example of loving the Lord and others when they were growing up with absentee parents. The significant caregiver was usually a grandparent, often a grandmother, who would bring them to Bible studies, read Bible stories and pray with them. As a result, each of them was able to unswervingly embark on the path of dedicating their lives to the Lord. A closer look reveals that many of them were born in the early 1980s in an atheistic country and a turbulent world situation. Some were from single parent homes where one parent either abandoned them or left the family for a job in distant city. Many experienced hardships because of a lack of basic provisions while growing up. Without the love and faithful example of God-fearing grandmothers, I wonder how these future young preachers would have understood the meaning of survival under God's watchful care.

1. BE INTENTIONAL FOR SUCH A TIME AS THIS

Recently, the wife of a pastor of a Chinese church shared that their church had resumed physical gatherings. During one fellowship time, a father and son attended. After the meeting, the pastor's wife went over to greet them and suddenly realized that the son was in fact the daughter of the family she had been familiar with! Later, she learned from the father that since his daughter believed that she grew up in a divorced family, she not only decided to change genders during the pandemic, but also undergo gender reassignment surgery. Her father's attempt to dissuade her was of no use. He had no choice but to let her do as she wished.

Such is the present evil days of our time—a generation forsaking God's covenant. This crooked and rebellious generation has abandoned the Word of the Lord so completely! Not only are self-serving people deviating from God's principles, but they do so defiantly! Looking at the news from around the world, there are illegal activities everywhere. Human morality has collapsed and become corruptible. When people's greed is not satisfied, they will be harmed by their own desires. In the 1970s in the United States, major feminist events launched the women's liberation movement. Now everyone emphasizes individual freedom that ignores discipline. Even the basic genders of man and woman are not subject to the control of the Master who created human life.

There are also frightening political factors, such as the controversial California law known as AB 2119. This new California law allows children as young as 12 to undergo gender reassignment treatment without parental consent. God is not unaware of the corrupt lives of people who have abandoned his Word. The Bible predicts that in the last days people will generally become worse and worse. People will have lost their moral standard, and the social atmosphere will become increasingly corrupt. "For then people will be self-absorbed, lovers of money, boastful, arrogant, slanderous, disobedient to parents, ungrateful, unholy in heart, unloving, unkind, slanderous, unable to control themselves, violent, unloving God, traitors to friends, self-willed, conceited, lovers of pleasure rather than lovers of God" (2 Tim. 3:2-4).

Alas! This is the dynamic of moral corruption in the generation in which our children and grandchildren will grow up! Therefore, the responsibility of deliberately educating the next generation with God's biblical mandate is even more critical and urgent!

How can we stand by and do nothing for the well-being of the next generation? How can we let the culture take its course and allow this immorality to seep into the lives of our children's children without being troubled by it? Shouldn't this drive us to our knees to pray for our next generation, asking God for His mercy and protection? As Christian grandparents, we must not only keep our faith, but also intentionally live out the truth with a mission, so that the Lord's grace can shine and be passed down from generation to generation!

Here is an example of how I as a baby boomer and grandmother, intentionally passes on Christian values to a Gen Alpha granddaughter, while reading books together. My friend, who is a counselor and a children's book author herself, sent me a set of her children's books, the Bee Series.[104] In these books, she creatively explores different areas of family living. She gives interesting and age-appropriate explanations about practical aspects of daily life, hygiene, safety and how to deal with others at home, at school, and at play. The series uses

---

104 Joyce Piap-Go, *The Bee Series: Bee Patient*, (Manila: OMF Literature Inc. 2021).

the English word Bee as the theme word in the following ways: Bee Polite, Bee Healthy, Bee Kind, etc. Early childhood specialists assure us that reading aloud to young children contributes to their love of reading. Additionally, books like the Bee Series can guide children, cultivating wholesome virtues as well as imparting Christian values.

I was reading the book Bee Patient to my granddaughter when my daughter's mother-in-law, who is Caucasian, was around. She told me that she completely agreed with the content. Then she added, quite sadly and distressed, "It's a pity that the education here is teaching the opposite. Children here are told not to be patient and wait, but to act now!"

Hearing this, as grandparents, parents, uncles, and aunties, we must individually and unswervingly grasp the Lord's promises, and pray for those who come after us. Let us trust and obey God's Word and teachings, following them single-mindedly, and maintaining a daily relationship with the Lord. When godly grandparents and parents value continuous daily devotional time with the Lord and model authentic reverent Christian living in their talk and walk, then they are living out their faith. Such unwavering faith in our One True God, can be seen and felt by our children and grandchildren. By God's grace, this faith will be able to flourish in their hearts and minds, impacting the lives of those around us, and even influencing future generations.

2. COMMITMENT TO INTENTIONAL CHRISTIAN GRANDPARENTING

Earlier in this article, I mentioned that the Chinese Grandparenting Legacy Coalition was recently established. Amazingly, this organization has produced a three-volume Chinese book on Intentional Grandparenting: Passing the Faith from Generation to Generation within the last two years. Under the editorship of Amy Lin, about 20 Chinese Christian authors have worked together to produce these timely resources. This is truly an intentional and united effort with the generosity and encouragement coming from the founder of Legacy Coalition, Larry Fowler.

Fowler lists 14 factors that we cannot overlook when becoming an intentional Christian grandparent. These are unpacked using the word grandparenting as an acrostic word.[105]

---

[105] Larry Fowler. "14 Can't Overlook Factors", In *Equipping Intentional Grandparents Vol 1: Grandparenting Essentials,* (CA: Legacy Coalition, 2023), 10-25.

G – I will Guide Grandkids with Grace
R – I will Respect Parent Roles
A – I will Abound in My Affection
N – I will Nurture Their Nature
D – I will Deal with the Dilemma of Distance
P – I will Pray with Passion and Purpose
A – I will Adjust my Attitude
R – I will Restore Relationship
E – I will Excel in my Example
N – I will Number my Days
T – I will Tell Them my Testimony
I – I will Intentionally Influence
N – I will Never Neglect the Newest Generation
G – I will Give them the Gospel Now

As I type these 14 factors, I cannot help but being struck by the first-person imperative grammatical structure. It is so crucial and critical for us grandparents! In fact, I am even tempted to change the pronoun from 'I' for 'we,' as this task needs our combined and cohesive stand wherever we are.

Even as we deliberate how Christian grandparenting in a multi-generational situation can pave the way for the intentional passing on of our legacy of faith, we are also aware that grandparenting is not only filled with many joys, but it can also be filled with unexpected pain and problems. Relational tensions can exist in parent and adult child interactions, not to mention brokenness and pain related to grandparenting restrictions, adult prodigals, marital separation, divorce, blended family dynamics, as well as loss of relationship due to migration from wars or other catastrophic events. Grandparenting woes are being addressed, nonetheless, with great resources to provide hope no matter what the situation is.[106]

---

106 Larry Fowler, *Overcoming Grandparenting Barriers: How to Navigate Painful Problems with Grace and Truth.*, gen ed., Josh Mulvihill. (Bloomington, MN: Bethany House Publishers, 2019).

CONCLUSION

There is indeed a vital call for Christian grandparents to take full advantage of the opportunities given by God to live out and share their thriving faith with their children and grandchildren. With pressure from this fast-paced lifestyle, adult children are already experiencing the stress of balancing two careers and successful child-rearing. Christian grandparents can be intentional by coming alongside their children (devoted believers or not), to impart the Christian values and faith, for this generation and next generation.

Whoever you are, or whatever generation classification you may be, come, join this fruitful journey, and pass on our faith legacy. Then we can rejoice with our Heavenly Father, and our Lord Jesus Christ as we see our children and their children's children, walking in the way of the Holy Spirit!

SELECTED BIBLIOGRAPHY

Fowler, Larry. *Overcoming Grandparenting Barriers: How to Navigate Painful Problems with Grace and Truth.* General Edited by Josh Mulvihill. Bloomington, MN: Bethany House Publishers, 2019.

——. "14 Can't Overlook Factors." In *Equipping Intentional Grandparents Vol 1: Grandparenting Essentials.* CA: Legacy Coalition, 2023, 10-25.

Kasasa. *"Boomers, Gen X, GenY, Gen Z and Gen Z Explained."* Blog posted June 22, 2023. Online: https://offer.kasasa.com/blog/boomers-gen-x-gen-y-gen-z-and-gen-a-explained. Accessed January 29, 2024.

McLeod, Saul. *"John Bowlby's Attachment Theory."* Dated Jan 24, 2024. Online: https://wellbeingscounselling.ca/the-4-styles-of-attachment/. Accessed February 5, 2024.

——. "Mary Ainsworth: Strange Situation Experiment & Attachment Theory." Dated Jan 17, 2024. Online: https://www.simplypsychology.org/mary-ainsworth.html. Accessed January 30, 2024.

Pew Research Center. *"The Demographics of Multigenerational Households."* Online: https://www.pewresearch.org/social-trends/2022/03/24/the-demographics-of-multigenerational-households/. Accessed January 30, 2024.

Piap-Go, Joyce. *The Bee Series: Bee Patient.* Manila: OMF Literature Inc, (2021).

Shao, Rosa C. *"Rethinking the Faith Legacy."* Family Series: Intentionally Christian Grandparents- Passing on Faith Through the Generations. Edited by Amy Lin. Taipei: Pure Nard Publishing House, (2023): 90-118.

To, Sharon. *"Practical Examples of Attachment Relationships."* Family Series: Intentionally Christian Grandparents- Passing on Faith Through the Generations. Edited by Amy Lin. Taipei: Pure Nard Publishing House, (2023): 119-133.

Well Beings Counselling. *"The 4 Styles of Attachment."* Online: https://wellbeingscounselling.ca/the-4-styles-of-attachment/ Accessed February 5, 2024.

Do Not Abuse Seniors Nor Exclude Us From the Family Circle

Sadiri Joy Tira

In their soon-to-be-released book, co-authored with her husband, Joseph Shao, Rosa Shao has written a compelling chapter about how the older generation prepares the younger to receive the baton (the chapter is titled "Intergenerational Missions: Passing our Faith Legacy to the Next Generation"). Joy Recla as well, has written a powerful paper on three key Biblical characters and their formation towards leadership (the paper is titled "From Womb to Tomb: Generational Missiology in the 21st Century and Beyond").

Now, the younger generation who benefited from the tender loving care (TLC) of their parents and grandparents must reciprocate this by honoring and caring for their senior loved ones: "Children, obey your parents because you belong to the Lord for this is the right thing to do. Honor your father and mother. This is the first commandment with a promise. If you honor them, things will go well for you and you will have a long life on the earth." (Ephesians 6:1, compare with Exodus 20:12 and Deuteronomy 5:1).

Remember that your grandparents and parents are your family "roots, tradition and history." The Lord promised to the seniors: "Even to your old age and gray hairs I Am He, I am He who will sustain you. I have made you and I will carry you. I will sustain you and I will rescue you" (Isaiah 46:4).

Elder abuse is a serious global issue. According to a UN Report (2023) one out of six among 60-plus-year-olds are victims of abuse. This number will rapidly increase as the global population increases in age. This problem exists in both developed and under develop countries due to the aging population and a lack of leadership. Educators don't properly educate the younger generation!

In Canada, some cases are classified as crime. In Alberta (Canada), where I live, it is estimated that one out of 10 seniors are victims of elder abuse (Government of Alberta: Let's Talk About It). There are six common types of elder or senior abuse:

1. Physical: hitting causing physical harm.
2. Emotional and psychological abuse: name calling, false accusations and threat.
3. Sexual: forcing sex without the individual's consent.
4. Neglect or abandonment by caregivers: withholding or neglecting medication as required by medical experts.
5. Financial exploitation: stealing financial and property assets.
6. Healthcare fraud and abuse.

(Any of this abuse must be reported to the authorities: Seniors' Abuse Helpline, Edmonton Area 760-454-8888).

How many evangelical congregations are adequately responding? How many Christians are aware of this issue? The Apostle Paul instructed the believers to help the "faint hearted or downcast and the weak" — especially seniors (I Thessalonians 5:14-15).

The old folks are vulnerable and powerless to abuses. Their prayers should be like the prayer of Jehoshaphat: "O God we are powerless ... What do we do, we do not know what to do, but our eyes are on You" (II Chronicles 20:12).

If I were to pastor a local church or congregation again, I would do my best to educate my parishioners. I would lead the congregation to have a "Senior's Day" as a regular church event; I would invite community public health experts to conduct a congregational event (seminar); I would lead the church leaders to visit seniors' homes to pray and serve them practically; and I would mobilize many Christian lawyers to advocate and defend the victims of abuse. One of the most needy mission fields in the Northern Hemisphere is the seniors home; I would regularly challenge younger leaders to serve as counsellors and chaplains in nursing and senior's homes.

In July 2020 at the height of Covid 19 pandemic I had a severe and life threatening stroke that changed the course of my journey! The Healer healed me and the merciful Creator extended my life; the Master reassigned my field work where I still serve our Triune God! My wife and I now are "permanent residents" of a seniors home! Here we meet the Octogenarians and Nonagenarians most of whom are Eurasian immigrants. They came to Canada after World War II. They are now old widows and widowers. They are weak, broke and broken, lonely, isolated and even neglected by their own children and grandchildren.

Six individuals are to be noted (for their privacy, their real names are changed):

- George is 95 years old — a wealthy old man and former businessman! But now with limited vision he cannot drive anymore. He told me: "My son doesn't visit me. He steals my money! I have no more money in my bank account. I am broke, I can't even buy a pair of socks."
- Peter, age 78, was a medical doctor in another province of Canada. He had a successful practice until he had stroke in 2021 (like me, he was a victim of an especially cruel stroke). His daughter moved him to Edmonton and he doesn't know where she is now. His hearing and memory were impacted greatly by the stroke. He is now a very confused man. He can't put on his underwear and none of his friends visit him. He has to beg for a ride from his

daughter if her schedule allows her to take him to the medical clinic.
- Richard, 85, is a former lead priest of a huge congregation. Before his death we talked many times about theological issues, for example, the Second Coming of Jesus Christ, his belief of a purgatory, the Virgin Birth, Judgment Day, and Heaven. One day after our dinner at the seniors home he prayed to Jesus and accepted that He is the only way to God. Rev. Richard got ill and he was taken to the hospital. He stayed there for a couple of weeks before he died suddenly. While he was in the hospital nobody cared to visit him. For several weeks afterward I thought about our providential meetings, especially our divine-appointment dinner. He was a peaceful and happy man after that dinner. He wrote me and my wife thanking us for our friendship and prayers.
- Aurora, 88, a widow for over two decades, was living by herself in her apartment before moving in at the senior's home. Almost every week her children visited her, assuring her of their love and care for her. She was surrounded by her children and grandchildren until her last breath!
- Joe, 79, is an octogenarian but he can't walk without someone assisting him. He is Peruvian and was a mechanical engineer who immigrated to Canada 25 years ago. He is an adherent of the Pentecostal movement. Not even one of his children and grandkids come these days to give him his favorite Tim Hortons coffee.
- My wife and I are the youngest in our seniors home! We are privileged to have friends and family members who love us. They regularly visit us, to pray for us and have lunch or dinner with us.

We are here at the seniors home for a purpose. We continue to be missional. We visit these folks who are older than us. We lead weekly Bible studies that are officially endorsed by the management; together with some of them we pray for missionaries and pastors and the young people to serve the Master in His vineyard. We visit these elderly folks in their apartment to pray for them and to assure them of God's love (Romans 8:28-33). They are happy when we call them

Auntie or Uncle, Papa or Mama. We open the dining room door for them to dine with us and spend time during social events.

Some of them pray, go to their local church, and continue to financially support missionaries. However, every day I see many of them sitting in a corner or under the tree alone in tears ... only God understands those tears: "You keep track of all my sorrows. You have collected all my tears in your bottle. You have recorded each one to your book" (Psalms 56:8). All of these seniors are waiting for their own time to be ushered into their own tomb!

There are times when I am also assaulted by loneliness, discouragement — the feelings of loss, betrayal and abandonment. But in times like this I fix my eyes to the author and finisher of our faith (Hebrews 12:2). I draw encouragement and strength to remember the good old days when I saw my children learning to walk, talk, going to school, church and reading books, picnicking in the park eating ice cream, climbing on my shoulders, whispering: "I love you Daddy." My hope is that I know and am assured that I will join my own grandparents and parents who are now in the City of God. Beyond my tomb is Heaven, our Fatherland, and in heaven there is no more pain, suffering, tears and crying (Revelation 21:1-4). My prayer is to hear the Master King Jesus; He will embrace me and declare "well done my good and faithful servant" Matthew 25:21). "Welcome home!"

Children, love your parents and grandparents. Do not cut them off from your family circle and your community. Do not isolate them nor keep distance from them. I appeal that you not let them carry heavy burdens alone and let them cry and drink their own tears from a shattered jar and broken glass!

Conclusion

Sadiri Joy Tira

The book I am writing, *From Womb to Tomb: Generational Missiology in the 21st Century & Beyond* is a germinal work by evangelical scholars and practitioners from the Philippines, Australia, Latin America, South Africa, the U.K, the U.S. and Ghana. The younger missiology students may bookmark it and learn from this volume to produce more resources to better understand their generation; like the children of Issachar who understand their times (1 Chronicles 12:32) they meet to partner and collaborate. I hope reading this book will result in effective ministry and missions strategy. May the younger leaders continue to effectively reach each generation as they rapidly change but the Great Commission of Jesus Christ remains true and unchanged.

Regional conflicts, ecological disasters, hunger, accelerated diasporic population movements — the question of our day is: "What is the new normal when it comes to defining unreached people groups in our now borderless world?" These hybrid, diasporic peoples are now highly mobile in our technology-heavy and inter-connected world (e.g. millennials, Gen Z or Gen B and the younger generation yet to come) but the seniors, baby boomers, octogenarians and nonagenarians remain; they need the Lord — the fresh touch of Jesus the Saviour! During our tumultuous days many are suffering beyond comprehension. Therefore, in concert let us pray "Even so Lord Jesus Come" (Revelation 22: 20).

Afterword

Matt Cook

During our time as church planters in Cusco, Peru, we welcomed several short-term missions groups from our supporting churches in the United States. Inevitably, these groups were composed of hardworking Christians of all ages, from teenagers to senior citizens. Cusco is located at 11,000 feet in altitude and often causes guests to experience some of the many symptoms of altitude sickness. Over time, we discovered that one's age or fitness level did not determine how one responded to the high altitude. Over the years, teenagers, middle-aged adults, and senior citizens all experienced serious altitude sickness that left them confined to their hotel room for the first part of the trip. Visitors randomly had different levels of altitude sickness, regardless of age. Apparently, altitude sickness does not show partiality. It doesn't matter how old you are; anyone could fall victim.

The point of this book is similar, but in a much more positive way. God's mission does not show partiality. It doesn't matter how old you are; anyone can participate. In fact, unlike altitude sickness, which does not necessarily impact every visitor to Cusco, Peru, God invites all Christians to participate in his mission, regardless of age. The book of Acts illustrates this most clearly. Intergenerational mission comes alive as Luke shares the narrative of bold women and men of a variety of ages proclaiming the Good News of Jesus. Paul's companions like Timothy and Luke were probably younger (20s or 30s), while Luke narrates nearly thirty years of Paul's ministry, from "young man" (Acts 7:58), to veteran missionary and hero of the faith. Philip the Evangelist witnessed to Samaritans and the Ethiopian Eunuch (Acts 8) and then lived long enough to witness his daughters use their prophetic gifts to proclaim to the good news more than twenty years later (Acts 21:9). From beginning to end and from old to young, the disciples in the book of Acts remind us that God desires to work through all Christians, regardless of age.

This book, *From Womb to Tomb*, is a fresh reminder of what Acts teaches us: God desires to work through all Christians, regardless of age. To my older brothers and sisters who are veteran missionaries and missiologists: you matter! Your years of experience and study serve as an impetus to the church and a new generation of missionaries. Younger generations need your encouragement and sometimes your gentle correction. Younger missionaries need you to equip them with your knowledge and inspire them with your stories. The church needs your continued work in churches and "mission fields," wherever life's circumstances have placed you. Please, keep using your missiological expertise in God's mission.

To my younger brothers and sisters, college students and new missionaries: you matter! Your youthfulness and vigor serve as an impetus to the church to continue mobilizing energetically and creatively. Ask veteran missionaries for their advice and training. Read the new resources that will carry the church into the future, but also read the classics in missiology. Older missionaries need your encouragement and inclusion. Please, keep using your energy and excitement in God's mission.

To those like me, college professors, missionaries, missions administrators: you matter! Your experience and hard work serve as an impetus to the church to continue mobilizing responsibly and wholistically. Both younger missionaries and older missionaries need you to serve them and include them. Amid all the busyness of academia or administration, build relationships with other generations that will encourage and mobilize Christians young and old.

Just as Jesus gave his Great Commission to a diverse group of apostles that consisted of fishermen, a Zealot, and a tax collector, he gives that same Commission to the modern diverse church that consists of young and old from every continent. May disciples of all ages, from womb to tomb, rise to the high calling of Jesus as He equips His church for mission from everywhere to everywhere!

List of Contributors

Nana Yaw Offei Awuku

Nana Yaw Offei Awuku serves as the global associate director for generations. In this role he leads the Lausanne Younger Leaders Generation initiative (YLGen). He was previously the Lausanne regional director for English, Portuguese, and Spanish-speaking Africa (EPSA) for over five years until September 2016.

Joseph Shao:

Dr. Joseph Shao is now the President Emeritus of the Biblical Seminary of the Philippines, after he served for 30 years as its President. He holds a PhD from the Hebrew Union College, Ohio. He is the 4th General Secretary of the Asia Theological Association (ATA). He received *"Qianbei"* (Senior Scholar) award at the International Congress of Ethnic Chinese Biblical Scholar. Currently, he is the Regional Secretary of ATA North America. Together with his wife Rosa, they now serve with the Global Mission Seminary in Irvine, California. They have three grown-up children, and six grandchildren.

Joy V. Recla:

Dr. Joy V. Recla has PhD with focus on the Old Testament and Semitic Languages from Fuller Theological Seminary, Pasadena, California. She is currently a faculty at the International Graduate School of Leadership in Quezon City, Philippines. She is married to Ricardo Recla and have three grown up sons.

Dr. Barbara Deutschmann:
Dr. Barbara Deutschmann is a PhD graduate and a distinguished scholar. She is an author and a post doctoral associate of Whitney College, part of the University of Divinity, Australia. Her research interest is on Gender.

Narry Santos:
Dr. Narry F. Santos is Associate Professor of Christian Ministry and Intercultural Leadership at Tyndale University in Toronto and Vice President of the Evangelical Missiological Society Canada. Narry has a PhD in New Testament (Dallas Theological Seminary, 1994) and another in Philippine Studies (University of the Philippines, 2006). He wrote several books, including *Family Relations in the Gospel of Mark* (Peter Lang, 2021) and *Slave of All* (Sheffield, 2003).

Jolene Erlacher:
Dr. Jolene Erlacher (Ed.D) grew up as a missionary kid. She is a next gen researcher, speaker, and consultant at www.leadingtomorrow.org. Her latest book, *Mobilizing Gen Z: Challenges and Opportunities for the Global Age of Missions* (William Carey Publishing) presents insights and strategies for engaging the next generation in mission. Jolene and her family live in North Carolina.

Micaela Braithwaite:
Micaela Braithwaite serves as communications strategist for the Lausanne Movement. She completed her honours degree in theology at the Baptist Theological College of Southern Africa, where she also taught a course in biblical languages. Micaela has previously served as a children's and youth pastor. Born and raised in Johannesburg, South Africa, she and her husband now live in the Channel Island of Guernsey.

Johann Uytanlet:
Johann Sven Lee Uytanlet is a Computer Science student at De La Salle University in Manila, Philippines. He is the son of Samson and Juliet Uytanlet.

Josephine Tan:
Josephine Tan is from Cebu, Philippines. She graduated Master of Science in Theology major in Biblical Studies from Asia Pacific Nazarene Theological Seminary in August 2020. She is passionate about Teaching Biblical Languages.

Alice Wulbern:
Alice Wulbern (not her real name) grew up in North Carolina, USA, and worked as a professional musician and college educator before being called to the mission field. She served in Latin America for 15 years and in Asia for 25 years in the areas of evangelism and discipleship, women's and children's ministries, leadership training, education, and TESOL. Now semi-retired, she continues teaching English to internationals in the U.S., and online to seminary students and others in Asia.

Alma Pinno Kisser:
Alma, turned 92 years old. She was born in Poland lived in Germany then immigrated to Canada. She is now a widow. She belongs to Nona-generation.

Rosa Shao:
Dr. Rosa Shao is a professor of Counseling at the Biblical Seminary of the Philippines, Manila, and Asia Graduate School of Theology, Quezon City, Philippines. She holds a PhD in Clinical Psychology and is a licensed counselor and a Certified Solution-Focused Therapist.

Sadiri Joy Tira:
Dr. Sadiri Joy Tira, DMiss, DMin is a Diaspora Missiology Specialist from Jaffray Centre for Global Initiatives, at Ambrose University. He was the Lausanne Movement's Senior Associate / Catalyst for Diaspora(2006-2018) and the Founding Chairman of Global Diaspora Network (2010-2015)

Matt Cook
Dr. Matt Cook is the Assistant Professor of Bible, Global Missions and World Religions, and is the Program Coordinator of the Doctor of Ministry program at Freed-Hardeman University. Prior to his role at FHU, Matt and his wife Charla were church planters in Cusco, Peru. Matt earned a PhD (2019) in Missions and World Religions from The Southern Baptist Theological Seminary. His research interests include diaspora missiology, contextualization, and missions pedagogy.

Sophie and Bishop Tira
Junior high school and elementary students in Canada. They are both active in their church and in school.

Appendix

Note:
Lausanne Generations Conversations
May 31-June 3; 2023
Biola University
La Miranda, California

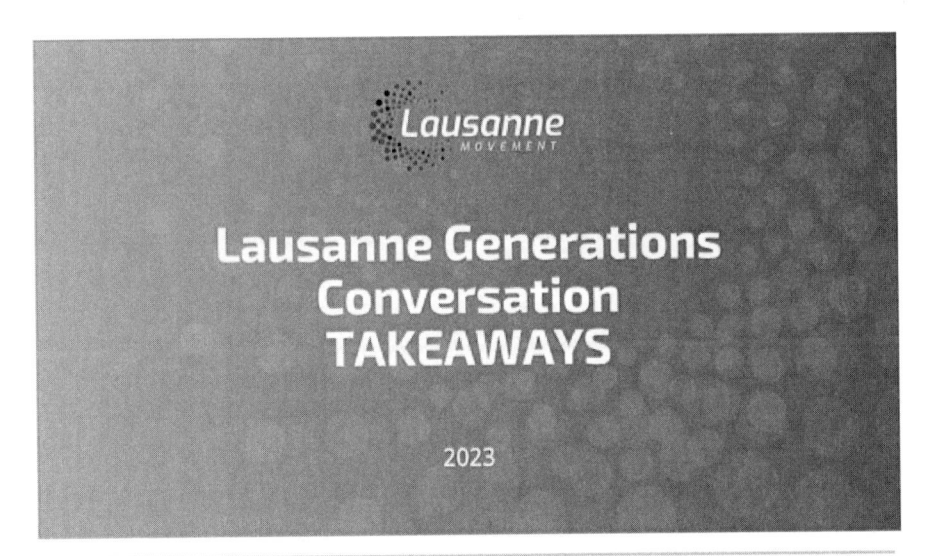

Lausanne Generations Conversation TAKEAWAYS
2023

Overview

As part of the Lausanne 4 journey, LGC23 was a unique on-site gathering of 106 Christian leaders from across generations (ages 18—81), geographies (41 countries), and missional interests.

LGC23 explored insights, models, and best practices for intentional intergenerational connecting, convening, communities, and collaboration for global mission throughout the Movement in the coming decades.

- 18-27 YEARS
- 28-40 YEARS
- 41-55 YEARS
- 56-70 YEARS
- 70+ YEARS

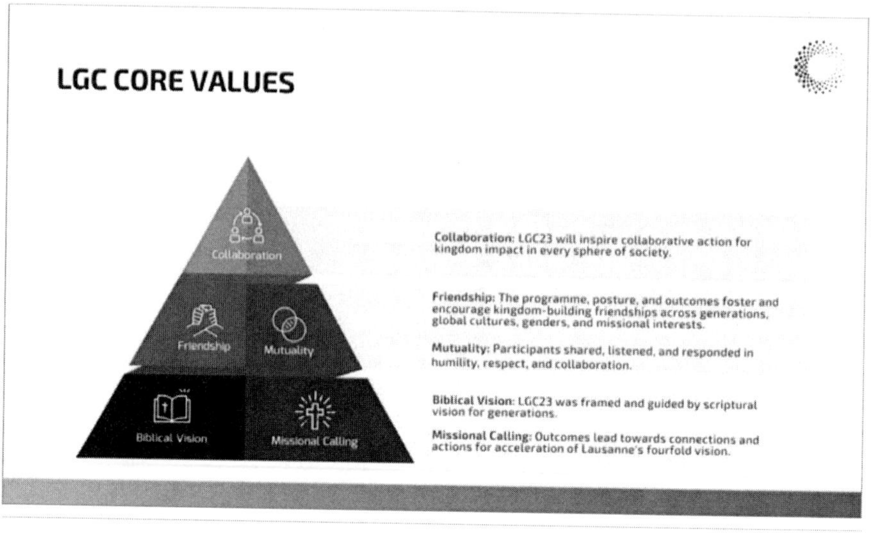

LGC CORE VALUES

- **Collaboration** (top of pyramid)
- **Friendship**, **Mutuality**
- **Biblical Vision**, **Missional Calling**

Collaboration: LGC23 will inspire collaborative action for kingdom impact in every sphere of society.

Friendship: The programme, posture, and outcomes foster and encourage kingdom-building friendships across generations, global cultures, genders, and missional interests.

Mutuality: Participants shared, listened, and responded in humility, respect, and collaboration.

Biblical Vision: LGC23 was framed and guided by scriptural vision for generations.

Missional Calling: Outcomes lead towards connections and actions for acceleration of Lausanne's fourfold vision.

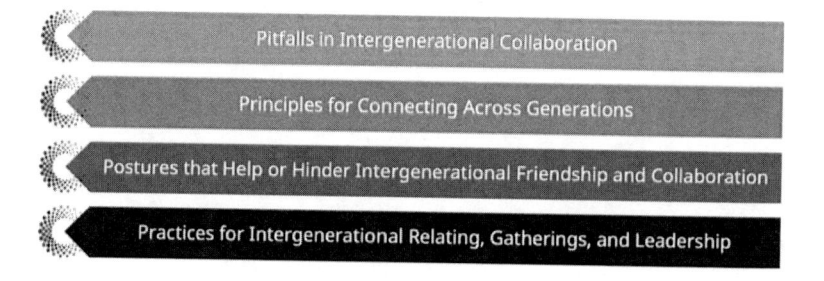

LGC TAKEAWAYS

- Pitfalls in Intergenerational Collaboration
- Principles for Connecting Across Generations
- Postures that Help or Hinder Intergenerational Friendship and Collaboration
- Practices for Intergenerational Relating, Gatherings, and Leadership

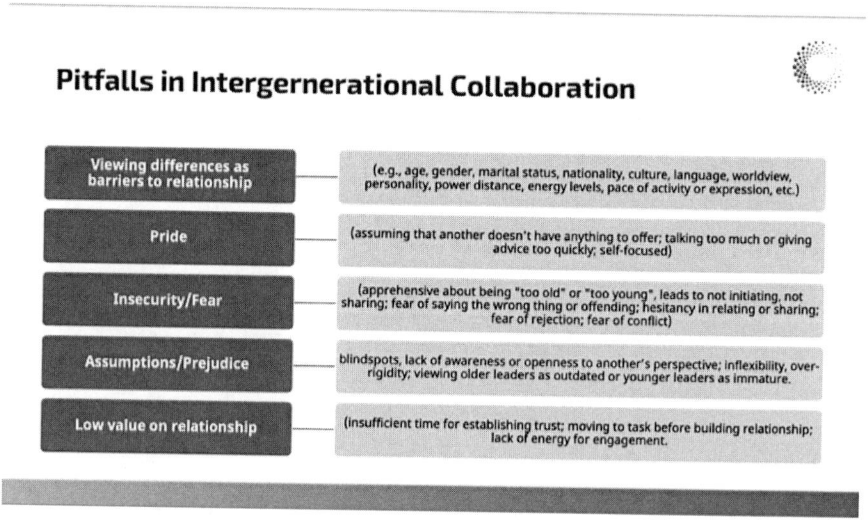

Pitfalls in Intergernerational Collaboration

Pitfall	Description
Viewing differences as barriers to relationship	(e.g., age, gender, marital status, nationality, culture, language, worldview, personality, power distance, energy levels, pace of activity or expression, etc.)
Pride	(assuming that another doesn't have anything to offer; talking too much or giving advice too quickly; self-focused)
Insecurity/Fear	(apprehensive about being "too old" or "too young", leads to not initiating, not sharing; fear of saying the wrong thing or offending; hesitancy in relating or sharing; fear of rejection; fear of conflict)
Assumptions/Prejudice	blindspots, lack of awareness or openness to another's perspective; inflexibility, over-rigidity; viewing older leaders as outdated or younger leaders as immature.
Low value on relationship	(insufficient time for establishing trust; moving to task before building relationship; lack of energy for engagement.

Principles for Connecting Across Generations

Missional friendships are both side-by-side and outward; intentionally developing relationships and engaging common interests for common goals.	Mutuality is made possible when there is trust, humility, respect, empathy, and reconciliation.	Leaders recognize gifts in others and make space for their development by delegating responsibility with corresponding authority.	Experienced leaders can bless emerging leaders through encouraging, empowering, and opening doors for them.	Appreciating what different generations have to offer strengthens collaboration.

Postures that Hinder or Help

Hinder		Help
• self-centered, assuming you don't need anything from a person of a different age • focus on accomplishments or titles • talking too much about self; "imperial style" • desire to teach or lecture	**Pride** / **Humility**	• approaching others with a willingness to learn or receive; • accepting that your way is not necessarily the right/best way; • holding own culture with an open-hand rather than superiority
• disregarding someone based on perceive difference; • not making room for another's opinion disregarding another's perspective • distrust	**Assumptions and Stereotypes** / **Openness**	• to relationship; • to sharing your story; • to different perspectives; • to learning; to receiving feedback; • empathy
• lack of listening; • ceding in conversation, not speaking; inattentive; • distracted by phone or work; • unavailable; • Unapproachable, monologues	**Disengagement** / **Curiosity**	• about another's experience; • showing genuine interest; • desire to learn
• not genuinely interested in relationship; • driving towards goal or task without awareness of others needs or desires.	**Focus on what another can give** / **Viewing another as an image bearer**	• a unique individual with value; • respect regardless of differences; • looking for the best in others

Postures that Hinder or Help

Hinder		Help
• uninterested; • unwilling to put in effort or relate with someone different	**Apathy** / **Love**	• relating to an individual with the desire to bless them and to be connected; • Genuine concern and interest; • kindness; • encouragement
• independent; • overly focused on own needs on agenda; • talking only with friends or peers	**Self-sufficiency** / **Reciprocity**	• to relationship; • to sharing your story; • to different perspectives; • to learning; to receiving feedback; • empathy
• writing someone off prematurely because of difference or mistake	**Impatience** / **Patience**	• in interactions; • recognizing that intergenerational relating may take time before payoff
• overly focused on previous relationships; • staying with own age or cultural group	**Exclusiveness** / **Inclusiveness**	• welcoming, friendliness, hospitality, making room for others in a conversation, smiling
• concern that you don't have anything to offer or won't be received; • hesitancy; • being cautious to share or disagree	**Insecurity** / **Willingness to risk**	• making mistakes, discomfort, dissonance, conflict, etc.

From Womb to Tomb

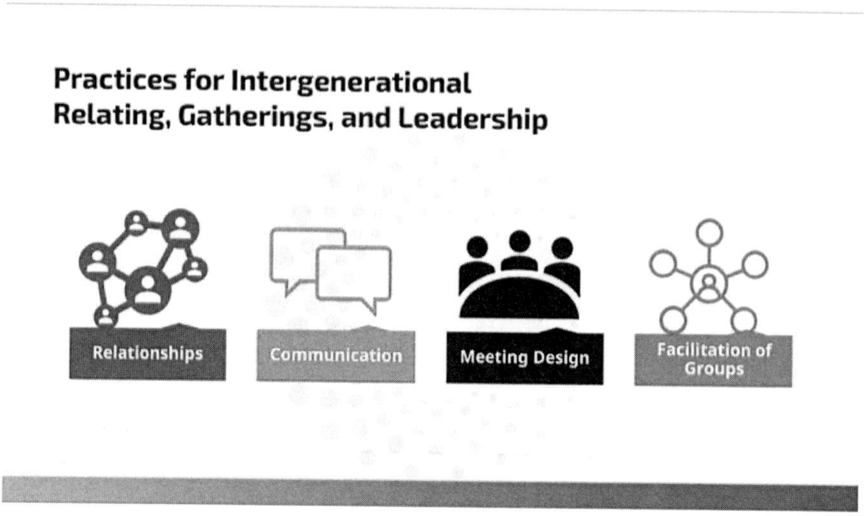

Practices for Intergenerational Relating, Gatherings, and Leadership

Relationships | **Communication** | **Meeting Design** | **Facilitation of Groups**

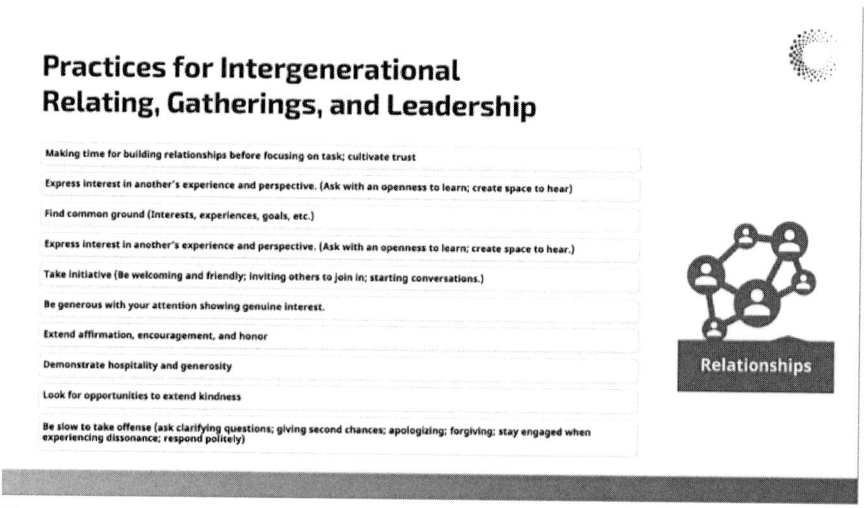

Practices for Intergenerational Relating, Gatherings, and Leadership

Making time for building relationships before focusing on task; cultivate trust

Express interest in another's experience and perspective. (Ask with an openness to learn; create space to hear)

Find common ground (Interests, experiences, goals, etc.)

Express interest in another's experience and perspective. (Ask with an openness to learn; create space to hear.)

Take initiative (Be welcoming and friendly; inviting others to join in; starting conversations.)

Be generous with your attention showing genuine interest.

Extend affirmation, encouragement, and honor

Demonstrate hospitality and generosity

Look for opportunities to extend kindness

Be slow to take offense (ask clarifying questions; giving second chances; apologizing; forgiving; stay engaged when experiencing dissonance; respond politely)

Relationships

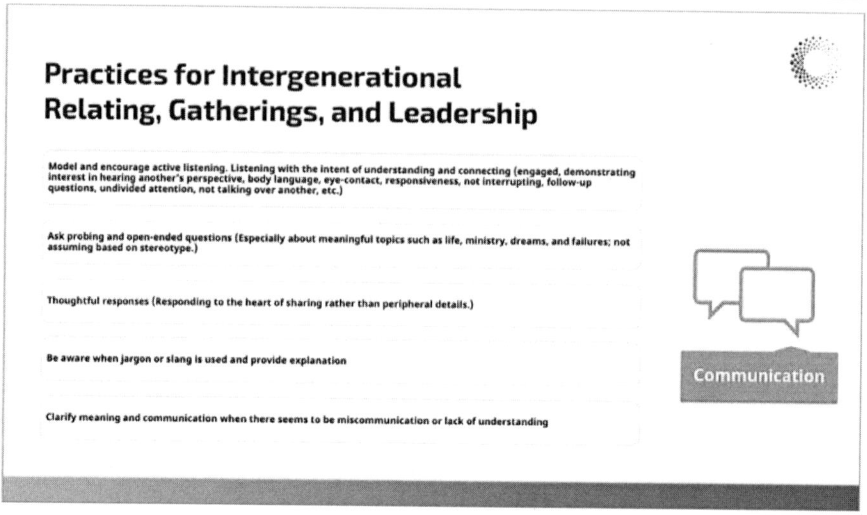

Practices for Intergenerational Relating, Gatherings, and Leadership

Model and encourage active listening. Listening with the intent of understanding and connecting (engaged, demonstrating interest in hearing another's perspective, body language, eye-contact, responsiveness, not interrupting, follow-up questions, undivided attention, not talking over another, etc.)

Ask probing and open-ended questions (Especially about meaningful topics such as life, ministry, dreams, and failures; not assuming based on stereotype.)

Thoughtful responses (Responding to the heart of sharing rather than peripheral details.)

Be aware when jargon or slang is used and provide explanation

Clarify meaning and communication when there seems to be miscommunication or lack of understanding

Communication

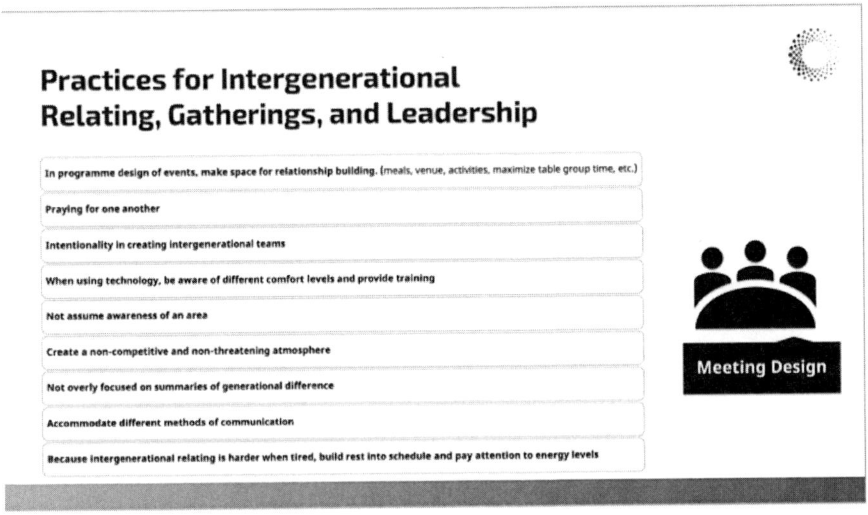

Practices for Intergenerational Relating, Gatherings, and Leadership

- In programme design of events, make space for relationship building. (meals, venue, activities, maximize table group time, etc.)
- Praying for one another
- Intentionality in creating intergenerational teams
- When using technology, be aware of different comfort levels and provide training
- Not assume awareness of an area
- Create a non-competitive and non-threatening atmosphere
- Not overly focused on summaries of generational difference
- Accommodate different methods of communication
- Because intergenerational relating is harder when tired, build rest into schedule and pay attention to energy levels

Meeting Design

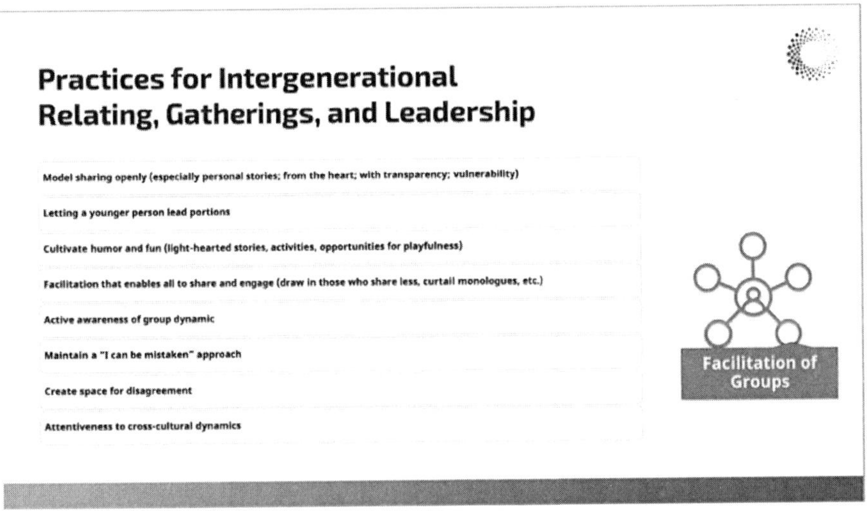

Practices for Intergenerational Relating, Gatherings, and Leadership

- Model sharing openly (especially personal stories; from the heart; with transparency; vulnerability)
- Letting a younger person lead portions
- Cultivate humor and fun (light-hearted stories, activities, opportunities for playfulness)
- Facilitation that enables all to share and engage (draw in those who share less, curtail monologues, etc.)
- Active awareness of group dynamic
- Maintain a "I can be mistaken" approach
- Create space for disagreement
- Attentiveness to cross-cultural dynamics

Facilitation of Groups

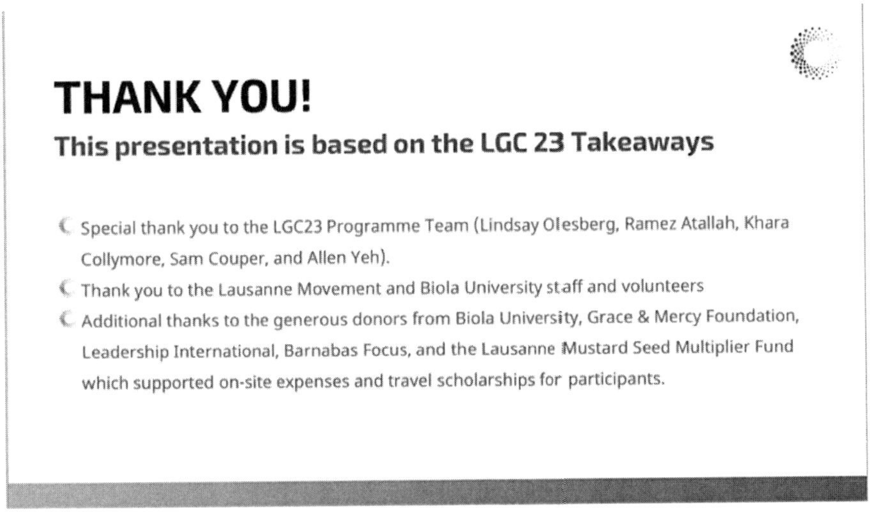

THANK YOU!
This presentation is based on the LGC 23 Takeaways

- Special thank you to the LGC23 Programme Team (Lindsay Olesberg, Ramez Atallah, Khara Collymore, Sam Couper, and Allen Yeh).
- Thank you to the Lausanne Movement and Biola University staff and volunteers
- Additional thanks to the generous donors from Biola University, Grace & Mercy Foundation, Leadership International, Barnabas Focus, and the Lausanne Mustard Seed Multiplier Fund which supported on-site expenses and travel scholarships for participants.

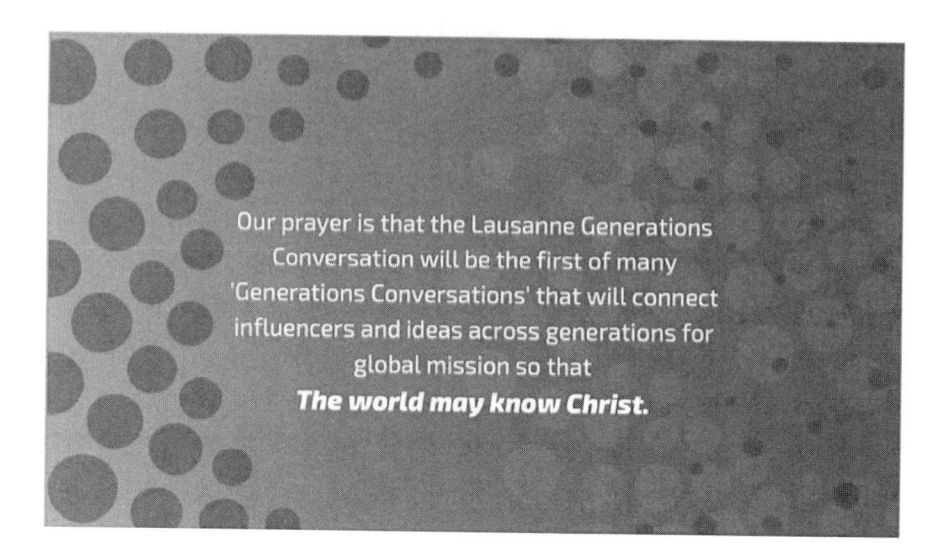

> Our prayer is that the Lausanne Generations Conversation will be the first of many 'Generations Conversations' that will connect influencers and ideas across generations for global mission so that ***The world may know Christ.***

Attribution:

This document was originally produced from the Lausanne Generations Conversation (June 2023) and is published here with permission. To learn more about the Lausanne Movement visit: WWW.LAUSANNE.ORG and to receive a free Lausanne Global Analysis bimonthly at: HTTPS://LAUSANNE.ORG/LGA